WORLD AT WAR

UNFORGETTABLE TALES FROM THE FIRST
AND SECOND WORLD WARS

WAR HISTORY JOURNALS

We shall go on to the end, we shall fight in France, we shall fight on the seas and oceans, we shall fight with growing confidence and growing strength in the air , we shall defend our Island, whatever the cost may be, we shall fight on the beaches we shall fight on the landing grounds, we shall fight in the fields and in the streets, we shall fight in the hills; we shall never surrender, and even if, which I do not for a moment believe, this Island or a large part of it were subjugated and starving, then our Empire beyond the seas, armed and guarded by British Fleet, would carry on the struggle, until, in God's god time' the New World, with all its power and might, steps forth to the rescue and the liberation of the old.

—Winston S. Churchill

CONTENTS

WWI

Cavalry officers on horseback, stubby tanks and rickety biplanes of the first world war, now seem part of a distant age. The casualties of this great war are so immense. It's easy to forget individuals caught up in this conflict. Most were civilians—farm and factory workers, civil servants, teachers—taken right from their everyday lives and plunged into a terrifying and lethal ordeal. This war was on too grand a scale to be fought by only professional standing armies.

The stories in this book are about ordinary men and women: soldiers, sailors, and aircrew caught up in great battles and campaigns. Those who survived with no apparent physical or psychological damage were tormented by what they'd seen and done. One British veteran recalled:

> *"It took us years to get over it. Years! Long after, when you were working, married, had kids, you'd be lying in bed with your wife and you see it all before you. Couldn't sleep. Couldn't lie still. Many's the time I've got up and tramped the streets till it came daylight. In many's the*

time I've met other fellows that were out there doing
exactly the same thing. Went on for years, that did."

For those that fought, the great war remained the most intense and vivid experience of their life. In the beginning of August 1914, the most powerful countries in the world declared war on each other. Known as the Central powers: Hungary, Austria and Germany lined up against the Allied forces: France, Britain and Russia along with their colonial empires.

As the Great War progressed, other nations were drawn into the conflict. Bulgaria and the Ottoman Empire joined the Central Powers. In contrast, Japan, China, Romania, the United States and Italy joined the Allies.

This was to be the first real-world war. It would ultimately involve countries from every continent. Most of the fighting took place in France and on the Eastern and Western fronts of Germany.

Crowds gathered at the news of the outbreak of war. They gathered in the grand squares of Europe's majestic cities. Each side anticipated great marches and heroic battles quickly decided. The Kaiser declared that his troops would be home by the time the leaves fell from the trees.

The British weren't as optimistic. It was often said that the war would be over by Christmas. Only a few farsighted politicians realized what was coming, including the British foreign secretary, Sir Edward Grey.

Britain declared war on Germany August 4th. Sir Edward Grey commented to a friend about Britain's entry into the First World War:

"The lamps are going out all over Europe. We shall not
see them lit again in our lifetime."

His remark held a deep significance. At the time, Britain was a stable, prosperous country with an enormous empire. This war would prove the grim reality of warfare in the 20th century and remove Britain as the most powerful nation in the world.

Nearly all other countries that participated in the war suffered as well. Half of all men in France between the ages of 20 to 35 were killed or severely wounded. The Hungarian-Austrian Empire disintegrated.

The Germans lost their monarchy after the war and were on the brink of a communist revolution. The war eradicated the Russian monarchy and brought the communist Bolsheviks to power. With them came 70 years of brutal, totalitarianism oppression. The Russians still suffer from the horrible consequences of the first world war.

The United States was one of the few countries to emerge a stronger nation. By 1919, the US had become the wealthiest, most powerful nation on earth.

Apart from its consequences, there's something uniquely haunting about the first world war. The city crowds that gathered that August had no idea what the next four years had in store. The waste of life or what British statesman Lloyd George described as:

"The ghastly butchery of vain and insane offenses."

After the final shell had been fired and the last gas canister unleashed, there was nothing to show for it except over 21 million dead.

Known as the war that will end all war. It was such a gut-wrenchingly horrible conflict. Many hoped humanity would not be foolish enough to do it again. After the Versailles peace treaty officially ended the war in 1919, the proceedings were dismissed as a 20-year-old cease-fire by one of the leading participants, French commander Marshall Foch. By the early 1920s, people began to refer to the war as the first world war.

The causes of the war were many. The system of rival alliances between the different European powers had built up in the previous decades. Individual countries tried to bolster their security and ambitions with powerful allies. Although alliances provided some security, they also came with obligations.

The events that led to war were set in motion in June 1914, when the Serbian student named Gavrilo Princip assassinated the heir to the Austro-Hungarian throne, Archduke Franz Ferdinand. In retaliation, they declared war on Serbia.

Serbia was an ally of Russia. So, Russia joined the war against Austro-Hungary and all other rival nations tied to their respective alliances. They were dragged into the conflict, whether they wanted to be or not.

Why should a quarrel between Russia and Austria-Hungary over a little-known country in Eastern Europe automatically involve France, Germany and Britain?

It was because each was obliged to support the other in the event of war. There were other long-standing resentments. Britain maintained their power by having the world's greatest fleet. So, when Germany began to build a fleet to rival the Royal Navy, relations between these two countries deteriorated fast.

The British and French had vast colonial empires. Germany, also prosperous and powerful, only had a few colonies and wanted more. They all joined in the fighting to maintain or improve their position in the world.

The reason the conflict was so horrific is easier to

explain. The war occurred at a moment in the evolution of military technology when weapons to defend a position were much more effective than the weapons available to attack it. The development of trench fortifications, barbed wire, machine guns, and rapid-fire rifles made it is simple and straightforward for an army to defend its territory. An army attacking well-defended territory had to rely on its infantrymen, armed with only rifles and bayonets—and they were to be slaughtered in the millions.

All the generals involved in the war had been trained to fight by attacking, so that's what they did. They'd been trained that horse cavalry was one of the greatest offensive weapons. Cavalry—still armed with lances, as they had been for the previous two thousand years, took part in a few battles, particularly at the start of the war.

These elite troops were quickly massacred. The tactics of Alexander the Great, Genghis Khan and Napoleon, all of who'd used cavalry to great effect, were no match for the industrial scale killing power of the 20th century machine-guns.

There were other ugly additions to the new technology of warfare: poisonous gas, fighter and bomber aircraft, zeppelins, tanks, submarines and, especially artillery (field guns, howitzers, etc.). These weapons had reached a new pinnacle of sophistication. They were much more accurate and fired more rapidly than before. Over 70% of all casualties in the first world war were caused by artillery. Artillery could be used to attack and defend, gave neither side an advantage and made fighting more difficult and dangerous.

The war began with a massive German attack on France, known as the Schlieffen plan after its originator, Gen. Alfred Graf von Schlieffen. The plan called for the German army to wheel through neutral Belgium and seize Paris. The idea was to knock France out of the war as soon as possible. Apart from neutralizing one of Germany's most powerful rivals, this would have two other advantages. First, it would deprive Britain of a base on the continent from which to attack Germany. Second, with their enemies to the West severely disadvantaged, Germany could concentrate on defeating the much larger Russian army to the East.

The fighting in late summer and early autumn of 1914 was among the fiercest in the war. Both sides suffered huge losses. At the battle of the Marne, the German advance was halted less than 15 miles from Paris. By November, the Armies had become bogged down in opposing rows of trenches, stretched from the English Channel down to the Swiss border. Give or take the odd few miles here and there, the front line remained the same for the next four years.

At Germany's eastern border, its armies won crushing victories against vast hordes of invading Russian troops in late August and early September. They prevented the Russian steamroller from overrunning their country. From here on, the German army gradually advanced eastwards. In 1915, there was an attempt by British and Australian Army Corps troops to attack the central powers from the South through Gallipoli in Turkey. The strategy was a disaster. Between April and December 1915, around 200,000 men were killed trying to gain a foothold in this narrow, hilly peninsula.

By 1916, the war that was supposed to end by Christmas 1914, look liked it would last forever. The Germans launched an attack on the fortresses of Verdun in February. Their strategy was a success in some ways. The French army lost 350,000 men and never recovered. The Germans suffered over 300,000 casualties as well, and the French held onto the fortresses.

On May 31st, 1916, the German fleet challenged the British Royal Navy in the North Sea, at the battle of Jutland. In an all-out confrontation, 14 British ships, and 11 German ships were lost. If the British Navy had been destroyed, Germany would undoubtedly have won the war.

Island Britain would have been starved into submission, as cargo ships would have been unable to sail into British waters without being sunk. The British may have lost more ships, but the German Navy never ventured out to sea again, and the British naval blockade of Germany remained intact.

On July 1, 1916, another great battle began. The British launched an all-out attack on the Somme, in northern France. The British commander in chief, Field Marshal Haig, was convinced that a massive assault would break the German front line. This would enable him to send in his cavalry and allows troops to make a considerable advance into enemy territory.

The attack failed in the first few minutes and 20,000 men were slaughtered in a single morning. The battle of the Somme continued to drag out for another miserable five months.

By 1917, a numb despair settled on the fighting nations. With appalling stubbornness, Field Marshall Haig launched another attack on the German lines–this time in Belgium. Bad weather turned the battlefield into an and impenetrable mud bath. Between July and November, when the assault was finally called off, both sides had lost a quarter of a million men.

Two other events in 1917 had massive consequences for the outcome of the war. The Russian people suffered terribly and in March, the revolution forced Czar Nicholas II to abdicate. In November, the radical Bolsheviks seized power and imposed a communist dictatorship on their country. One of the first things they did was to make peace with Germany.

The Bolsheviks assumed that similar revolutions would sweep through Europe, especially Germany. They believed that Germany would soon be a fellow communist regime who'd treat Russia more fairly. They agreed to a disadvantageous peace treaty in March 1918. Germany took vast tracts of land from the Russian Empire—Poland, Ukraine, the Baltic states and Finland. For Germany, this was a great victory. Not only had they added a vast chunk of territory to the eastern border, they could now concentrate all their forces on defeating the British and French.

But despite the successes, events were conspiring against Germany. After the battle of Jutland failed to win them dominance of the seas, Germany had drifted into a policy of unrestricted submarine warfare. German U-boats attacked any ship heading for Britain—even those belonging to neutral nations.

It was an effective strategy, but it backfired. The submarine attacks caused outrage overseas, especially in the USA, and became one of the main areas of how America turned against Germany. Pres. Woodrow Wilson brought his country in on the side of the allies on April 6, 1917. Still, it wasn't until the summer of 1918 that the American troops began to arrive on the Western front in great numbers.

The timing could not have been worse for the German army. The Ludendorff offensive, named after German commander Erich Ludendorff, beginning March 21, 1918. Twenty-six divisions broke through weary British and French troops on the Somme and swept onto Paris. For a while it looked as if Germany would win the war on the Western front as well as the Eastern front. So alarmed were the British that Field Marshal Haig issued an order to his troops on April 12 commanding them to stand and fight until they were killed:

"With their backs to the wall and believing in the justice of our cause, each one of us must fight to the end."

The Ludendorff offensive turned out to be the last desperate fling of the dying Army. Faced with stubborn British resistance and fresh, eager American troops, the German advance ground to a halt. The German army had no more to give, at home, the German population starved after four years of the Royal Navy blockade. Germany was on the verge of a revolution in August 1918.

The Allies made a massive breakthrough against the German front lines in northern France and began to make a relentless push toward the German border. Facing mutiny among his armed forces, revolution at home, and the inevitable invasion of home territory, the Kaiser abdicated. The German government called for an armistice–a cease-fire on November 11, 1918.

The fighting continued right up to the last day. In his memoirs, Gen. Ludendorff recalled the situation:

"By November 9, Germany, lacking any firm guidance, bereft of all will, robbed of her princes, collapsed like a pack of cards. All that we had lived for, all that we had bled four long years to maintain, was gone."

Although there were wild celebrations in allied cities, many the soldiers on the Western front took the news with a weary shrug. The guns fell silent. Weeds and vines gradually crept over the desolate battlefield, covering the withered trees and ravaged fields, turning the blackened earth to a pleasanter green. Crude, makeshift burial grounds were eventually replaced by towering monuments and magnificent cemeteries.

Many of those killed found a final resting place among long rows of marble crosses, each one with the name, rank and date of death engraved upon it. Others, whose torn remains were incomplete and unrecognizable, were buried under crosses marked known unto God.

It would be another 10 or 15 years before the charred trucks, shell carriages and tanks were taken away for scrap, and the shell holes filled in. By the time war broke out again in 1939, much of the land was being farmed again. But the faint smell of gas still lingered in corners. Rusting rifles and helmets still littered the scarred ground and shell cases, shrapnel fragments and bones could still be tiled from the battlefield of northern France.

TALL TALES OF THE ANGEL ARCHERS

Early afternoon on August 24, 1914. It's been a nightmare couple of weeks waiting to intercept the German cavalry. I looked at the thunderous sky and was reminded of a verse from Revelations, "And the great dragon was cast out...And his angels were cast out with him." My present surroundings added to this mood.

I was in the Belgian mining town of Mons, a marshy area intersected with canals, and littered with towering trash heaps.

I was the captain of the 4th Dragoon guards in the BEF (British Expeditionary Force) and have been sent to France at the outbreak of war. We faced over a million German soldiers that were hell-bent on reaching Paris as part of general Schlieffen's strategy to win a quick victory.

In between marching for days on end, I faced moments of sheer terror when caught by advanced German units or artillery fire. When I had to command my men to stand and fight. They confronted hordes of enemy soldiers, advancing in ranks so thick, they seemed to resemble dark clouds sweeping through the green fields towards them. Soldiers fighting in such conditions suffer from a state of exhaustion unimaginable to most people. In such a state, they reported seeing imaginary castles on the horizon, towering giants and squadrons of charging cavalry in the far distance–all, of course, hallucinations.

Our losses have been catastrophic—an average BEF infantry battalion of 850 men would be left with barely 30 men by the time the German advance was halted, and the trenches set up. I feel like we're living in apocalyptic times. It was during one desperate retreat that one of the strangest stories of my adventures in the war arose: it was whispered that a host of angels had come to the aid of British troops at Mons.

Not only had Angels saved our soldiers from certain death, but then also struck down the attacking Germans. Extraordinary as this story was, it was widely believed for decades after the war ended.

During the early stages of fighting, the Army authorities allowed no real news out from the battlefield and, in consequence, wild and fancy stories began to circulate. War correspondent Philip Gibbs wrote that the press and public were so desperate to know what was happening that:

> "Any scrap of description, any glimmer of truth, wild statement, rumor, fairytale or deliberate lie, which reached them from Belgium or France was readily accepted."

The liars must've had a great time. In this feverish atmosphere, the story of the Angels of Mons spread like wildfire. Like all urban legends, it was always told second-hand. A friend learned of a letter from the front which mentioned, or an anonymous officer had reported—the legend blossomed from there. Sometimes a mysterious, glowing cloud was featured in the story. Sometimes it was a band of ghostly horsemen or archers or even one time it was Joan of Arc herself. But most the time, it was a host of angels that had come to rescue the beleaguered British troops.

Many wild stories from this time were the result of government propaganda. But this one was more innocent. It was a newspaper article in the September 29th edition of the London evening news, written by a freelance journalist. A mysterious fiction story, it told of a group of British soldiers at Mons, under attack and vastly outnumbered by German troops.

As the Germans advanced, and death seemed moments away, the soldiers muttered the motto–May St. George be present to help the English. According to the story:

"The roar of the battle died down in his ears to a gentle murmur. Then, he heard, or seemed to hear thousands shouting St. George! St. George! As the soldier heard these voices he saw before him, beyond the trench long line of shapes with a shining about them. They were like men who drew the bow and with another shout their cloud of arrows flew singing through the air towards the German host."

The story was a poet mixture. England's patron saint and ghostly Bowman, the spirits of those archers, perhaps, who'd won a famous English victory against the French and Agincourt in 1415. Maybe the story was believed to be true because it appeared in the new section of the paper—probably due to problems fitting it elsewhere. Or a simple misunderstanding by the designer, rather than any deliberate attempt to mislead its readers.

The original telling was absurd enough, but, in the weeks and months after it was printed, the retellings became even more ridiculous. British newspapers stoked a strange hysteria by reproducing illustrations. They showed pious British troops praying in the trench, as ranks of ghostly bowmen fire glowing arrows at the approaching Germans. It swept through the country, and the story evolved into the bowmen becoming angel archers.

The journalist never claimed his story had a grain of truth to it:

> "*The tale is sheer invention,*" he admitted. "*I made it all up out of my own head.*"

He was so embarrassed by the effect it had on the British public.

The authenticity of the story was still being debated decades after the war ended. In the late 1920s, when an American paper declared the Angels were motion picture images projected onto the clouds by aircraft. The idea was to spread terror among the British soldiers. Still, the plan backfired, and the British assumed the ghostly figures were on their side. This report took it for granted that the Angels had appeared. It was merely offering a logical, if extremely implausible, explanation for why they were seen. Even in the 1970s and 80s, Britain's Imperial War Museum was still being asked about the authenticity of the story.

Nowadays, it's easy to scoff at the foolishness of those who believe such stories. But the fact the tale was widely believed tells us much about the society that fought the war. I was lucky enough to survive, but thousands of other men had been killed in the opening months of this conflict.

For those that lost husbands or sons, there was a great

need for consolation. Stories like this brought reassurance to grieving relatives. It was especially pleasing to note that God was so obviously on the side of the British rather than the Germans. Other unlikely stories circulated throughout the war. Some were based on the usual far-fetched tales told by troops on leave from the trenches.

It was widely believed that a renegade, international band of deserters ran loose in no man's land, the territory that lay between the opposing trenches. These stories were deliberately fabricated by the British government propaganda unit, to bolster morale at home and lure America into the war.

Most of the time, German military forces behaved no better or worse than any other army. But, during the desperate early stage of the war, the German army dealt brutally with resistance from Belgian civilians to the invasion of their country.

Hostages were shot in villages massacred in reprisals. From the bones of such stories, British propaganda built a picture of the German people as a nation of godless barbarians. Huns was the term most often used after the fourth-century soldiers of Attila, who destroyed Rome and much of Italy.

Sometimes, this propaganda was ridiculous in its grotesque imagery. German soldiers, it was reported, had replaced the bells in Belgian church steeples with hanging nuns. Later in the war, stories were planted in the British press saying that the Germans had their own corpse factory. And the German soldiers killed in the fighting were sent there, so the bodies could be made into explosives, candles, industrial lubricants and boot polish.

The reaction such stories produced in Britain was sometimes equally bizarre. German dachshund dogs were stoned in the street. Shops with German immigrant owners were attacked and looted. The stories created an atmosphere of intense fear and hatred of the enemy—as they were intended to do. Many rushed to join the Army in the opening months of the war. They were convinced that they were fighting for civilization against the barbaric foe who would rape and mutilate their wives and children. If the Germans should ever cross the Channel and invade Britain.

After the war, people realized that much of the news concerning the war, and the German enemy had been outright lies. Newspapers would never be so openly trusted again. This attitude persisted into the early stages of the second world war. This meant that when the stories of German death camps first broke, they were widely disbelieved. It was too much of an echo of the corpse factory story, 20 years before.

CHRISTMAS IN THE TRENCHES

For most people, Christmas is a time of celebration. Plenty of food and drink, opening presents with the family and cheerfulness for the new year.

Now, try and imagine the feelings of men exhausted from four months of heavy fighting. Homesick, missing their wives and children, and spending Christmas Eve shivering and muddy in waterlogged trenches. Their lives lived in a dark world of cold, hunger and hatred.

Christmas sometimes works a strange magic, even in conditions like those in December 1914.

On Christmas Eve, the German guns on the Western Front fell silent soon after dark. No shells, no murderous chatter of machine-gun fire, not even an occasional wind of a sniper's bullet. The British soldiers followed their example.

It was a clear, cold night and the stars burned brightly. Silence fell over the trenches and created an eerie atmosphere. Then, along some sections of the trenches, the lookouts on the British side saw strange lights flickering, swinging along the German front line. Some shots were fired. But when officers peered through their binoculars, they were amazed to see that these lights were illuminated Christmas decorations. There were even some small Christmas trees hung with candles. At first, many soldiers were suspicious. After all, the British commander in chief, Field Marshal Haig ordered all units to be on alert for a German attack over Christmas and new year.

I heard German soldiers singing Christmas carols. Then some of the British soldiers began to sing carols. We serenaded each other with shared Christmas memories. Maybe it was because hearing these familiar songs led to the amazing events of the following day.

It was now dawn on Christmas morning and there was a thick mist over some sections of the front. But when it cleared, the most extraordinary scene revealed itself. All along no man's land, and in some places as far as I could see, soldiers walked out to meet the enemy.

They huddled around in small groups, usually with one who could speak the other's language. Sometimes French was the common language. Sometimes there wasn't any language at all. We just communicated with smiles and gestures. We swapped cigarettes, chocolate, whiskey, and beer. Sometimes I even noticed equipment exchanges: belt buckles badges, even helmets. Before the war, many Germans had worked in England. Some even gave letters to be mailed to friends or girlfriends.

Several men took photos, showing the groups of British and German troops huddled together, freezing but relaxed in other's company.

Meetings like these occurred when a truce was arranged among the officers to bury the dead left lying between the trenches. Burial parties stopped to talk to each other in other parts of the front, especially where opposing trenches were close. A soldier would simply call over, and promise not to shoot anyone if they would come out to meet them

I was a Lieutenant with the 133rd Royal Saxon Regiment. My soldiers had boldly walked into pockmarked land between the trenches to talk with the enemy. I was astonished when one of my Scottish soldiers ran up from his trench with a foot ball. Within moments there were two sets of goalposts and helmets on the frozen ground. I can still remember the game clearly. Even though there was a language barrier and the fact that the same men had been trying to kill us only the day before, it was a remarkably good-natured game.

Both sides played with a fierce determination to win but carefully followed the rules. Even without the advantage of a referee. The Germans were astonished to discover that our Scottish soldiers wore nothing underneath their kilts. Whenever a fierce tackle or a strong gust of wind revealed one of our Scotsman's buttocks, they would whistle like schoolboys.

The game went on for at least an hour and soon enough word filtered back to the local German high command. I heard the senior officers strongly disapproved of our game and the other junior officers were ordered to call their men back to the trenches immediately. Even though we couldn't finish the game, we still won by a score of three goals to two.

Not all the encounters were as friendly. Other matches were played with animosity. We set up a boxing match between two opposing regimental champions and it ended with the two men offering to finish each other off in a duel at one hundred paces.

On December 30, there was a Yorkshire battalion that received a message from their German counterparts, warning them that they would have to start firing. The message explained that German generals were coming to inspect them that afternoon, and they had to put on a show of aggression. When the British artillery battery was ordered to destroy the farmhouse behind the German lines on January 1st, they sent word to the Germans, warning them to leave the building.

French and the Belgian allied soldiers met their German counterparts in far fewer numbers, and not with the same harmony. Maybe it was because the Germans were fighting from French or Belgian territory and the feelings between opponents were more deeply felt.

Field Marshal French's warning of a possible German attack had been issued precisely because the Army high command feared that this type of contact with the enemy might happen. It wasn't unusual in earlier wars, for troops to fraternize with the enemy on Christmas Day.

In the last century, it wasn't unheard of for opposing generals to sit down at Christmas dinner together after a year of stalemate and bloody carnage.

The next year at Christmas, strict orders went out to both sides forbidding a repeat of the previous Christmas' goodwill:

> *"Nothing of the kind is to be allowed...This year. The artillery will maintain a slow gunfire on the enemy's trenches commencing at dawn, and every opportunity will be taken to inflict casualties upon any of the enemy exposing themselves."*

This was the order I received from the Col. of the British division. Not everyone took notice of this order. The fortunes of those who disobeyed were mixed. When an officer in the Coldstream guards, who went to shake hands with the German soldiers who came armed over no man's land, was sent home in disgrace. Other British troops who walked out to the German opponent were shelled by their own artillery.

In some places, the open mixing of the previous year was successfully discouraged. A British officer noted with grim satisfaction, when the Germans opposite them started to sing carols, the British shelled them with artillery. Still, some troops made friendly gestures to their enemies.

On one part of the front line, opposing British and German soldiers lit fires and oil drums with pierced sides, and placed them along the tops of the trenches, it was a wonderful sight. I shall never forget it.

As the war dragged on, this type of old-fashioned civility became unusual. The casualty rate mounted, those who survived lost many friends and became increasingly bitter about the enemy. By 1916 and 1917, these Christmas meetings were rare. Sometimes, it happened on isolated parts of the front. But for most soldiers, the Christmas tree seemed as distant and unlikely as an end to the war itself.

Senior officers on both sides give orders to step up artillery bombardment over the Christmas period. Ensuring any such fraternization would never be repeated.

ZEPPELIN RAID ON LONDON

On May 31, 1915, the enormous dark shadow of the German airship LZ–38 sailed over the clouds in London. It was the size of the oceangoing liner. It loomed through the sky at a steady 50 miles an hour. The deafening drone of four powerful engines made any conversation between my crew and myself, impossible.

Through gaps in the clouds, the city could be clearly seen. London citizens were not expecting any kind of attack. In the West End, lights of the streets and playhouses blazed brightly below. I'm sure the inhabitants of the capital felt completely safe.

The Western Front was far away. German warships usually attacked British coastal towns, because they lacked the range to hit this far inland. I looked around and felt pleased with myself. There wasn't a searchlight or anti-aircraft gun aimed at us before the first bomb was dropped.

I gave a curt nod to the bombardier close by in the control cabin, and we dropped over a hundred bombs on the city below. We watched from our lofty perch and observed the bombs exploding. It was an exhilarating display. Fires broke out and buildings collapsed. In all, over 42 people died or were seriously wounded that night—and there was worse to come.

We attacked in a zeppelin. A huge airship named after the German inventor, Ferdinand Graf von Zeppelin. He'd been flying these massive hydrogen field behemoths since 1897. They were the perfect weapon. Although they did little actual damage, the disruption that harmed morale was formidable. Whatever we raided, traffic ground to a halt. People stared with fear into the sky, and all-electric lights were extinguished.

When the bombs began to drop, people crouched in alleyways and cellars. They whispered in dread, in case their voices carried up to betray them. They were even afraid to strike a match to light a cigarette, in case the flare caught the attention of our zeppelin. Despite our huge size, we were invulnerable to the fighter plane. It couldn't fly high enough to attack us.

Even when improvements in aircraft design allowed fighters to reach an altitude of the zeppelin, they couldn't climb very quickly. We'd be long gone by the time any fighters got there. When we began our attack, twenty-six batteries of anti-aircraft guns were placed around London, and searchlights lit up the sky with their bright, rapier beams.

These guns were a new invention. The science of hitting flying machines, even ones as big as zeppelins, was complex. Hitting a moving target at that range and priming a shell to explode at a particular height, was still a deadly art yet to be perfected.

When war first broke out, the German Kaiser, Wilhelm

II wouldn't allow zeppelins to be used over England. He was closely related to the British Royal family, and he knew that bombing from the air would bring civilian casualties and severe family disapproval. It became apparent that the war wouldn't be over quickly. It turned into a dreary stalemate with no end in sight. The Kaiser's own generals persuaded him it was his duty to use every advantage Germany had.

In early January 1915, the first zeppelins appeared over the East Coast of Britain, and we brought massive disruption and anxiety. Even in this early stage of the war, the only threat the zeppelin crew faced was the weather. Something so large would be vulnerable to a strong wind. Zeppelins crashed in storms.

Nothing the enemy threw at us had any effect. The British had to rely on the network of human spotters placed along the coast. It was nearly the same as they had done for the arrival of the Spanish Armada during the time of Queen Elizabeth I. But zeppelin spotters had an advantage of being able to report their sightings by telephone rather than a chain of bonfires.

They also use the cumbersome device called the ortho-phone—a huge, trumpet-like listening apparatus that was designed to detect the distant drone of the zeppelin's engines. As the war dragged on, the design of fighter aircraft and antiaircraft guns advanced

In 1914, The rickety biplanes could barely fly across the English Channel. But by 1916, the British had developed anti-aircraft guns capable of hitting our vast slow-moving zeppelins. They armed the aircraft with incendiary bullets, fired from machine guns mounted above the plane's cockpit. These projectiles glowed white-hot when discharged and were intended to set fire to our highly flammable zeppelins.

Our zeppelin crews carried no parachutes. We only had a certain amount of weight that these huge machines could lift into the air. Fuel and bombs were always given priority over our crew safety. If our zeppelin ever caught fire, we had no chance of escape. But these weapons endangered the British pilots as well, often exploding when used.

Other zeppelin crews reported near misses and lucky escapes from anti-aircraft fire. It was decided that night attacks would be safer. As it turned out, they were also tremendously harmful. It was the threat of attack more than any actual damage done, that caused the most harm.

If zeppelins were detected in the night sky, they'd extinguish the lights below. It was a blackout, and it caused a massive disruption and inconvenience for factories and other local industries. Our zeppelins sent out huge powerful flares, we hoped to find our way by briefly illuminating the land below. Still, when we launched these flares, we gave our position away to night fighter pilots and vigilant anti-aircraft batteries.

As our zeppelins became more vulnerable to attack, we adopted other methods of defending ourselves. We mounted machine guns on top of our hulls. It took a special kind of courage and stamina to man them. We would tether a gunner to this precarious position and expose him to both the machine guns of attacking fighter planes and the freezing high-altitude temperatures. If our gunner was injured or overcome by either, it was impossible to rescue him.

We created an ingenious device to protect our crew called the cloud car. It was shaped like a fairground rocket ride. The car and its single passenger would be lowered from the interior of the zeppelin by a long cable that dangled its load half a mile below. The zeppelin would lurk inside the thick cloud, safely concealed from the air and aircraft attack. While the cloud car dangled in the clear air beneath, too small to be seen in the vastness of the sky.

It's passenger, would be in communication with the zeppelin via a telephone line, and then direct the ship towards its target.

It was a dangerous job. One cloud car passenger was smashed to death on the cliff when the zeppelin flew too low over the coast. If the cable snapped or jammed, the cloud car passenger was at the mercy of any enemy warplane that spotted him. He could also be hit by bombs dropped from his own zeppelin. But, despite these additional dangers, there is no shortage of volunteers for cloud car duty. This was mainly because the passenger was allowed to smoke. Smoking was forbidden in the zeppelin because it's highly flammable and has a hydrogen packaged fuselage.

For 2 years, our zeppelins roamed at will over Britain. Our greatest enemy was the weather or occasional structural failure. But on September 2, 1916, everything changed. That evening the crew German airship SL–11 and Lieut. William Robinson, a pilot of the 39th squadron of the home defense wing of the Royal Flying Corps, was about to earn their place in history.

* * *

It was a wet and dreary day. There were nineteen airships from the German Navy and Army services that took to the air and began the long journey through the darkening skies over the North Sea. This was the largest fleet of airships so far assembled by the Germans, and their target was the British military headquarters in London.

Not all were zeppelins. Half the fleet had been manufactured by rival airship firm made from wooden, rather than light metal frames. These airships were equally formidable. The SL–11 was 570 feet long and 70 feet high and could carry a similar number of bombs.

We now had a new anti-zeppelin weapon in our arsenal. We'd been using incendiary bullets against airships for as long as we'd been trying to shoot them down. These bullets have proved themselves ineffective. New, more powerful incendiaries had been developed, and the results have been disastrous. These new types of bullets were prone to explode in the weapon firing it, and we'd lost nearly a dozen British warplanes while trying to use it.

As night fell, radio operators at listening stations picked up a noticeable increase in German wireless communications. This suggested a massive raid was in progress. The spotters along the coast scanned the skies for any incoming airships. By 10 o'clock that evening, the airship fleet had been detected approaching the Norfolk coast. The massive sound of its combined engines hinted at the size of the attack.

London's antiaircraft gun batteries and airfields were alerted. Over on the Suttons farm airfield 20 miles southwest of London, I prepared my biplane for takeoff. These lumbering two-seater planes were typically used as reconnaissance aircraft. Their broad wings and powerful engines enabled them to fly higher than many of the faster and more maneuverable fighters in the Royal Flying Corps. The BE2s mission was to intercept zeppelins. They usually only carried one crew member rather than two; the lack of extra weight allowed the plane to climb higher. I flew off into the moonless sky just after 7:30. That night I was one of six pilots to try my luck in the dangerous skies of London.

It took an entire hour for my BE2 to reach 10,000 feet altitude. I peered through the velvet sky, hoping to spot a looming black hole, but I saw nothing. I even switched off the engine, hoping to hear the approaching airships.

It was just after one in the morning, and I spotted this zeppelin, it was the LZ-98. I turned to attack and fired a hail of bullets into the vast body of the airship. Nothing happened. As soon as the crew realized they were under attack, they executed the standard zeppelin procedure. The LZ–98 rose swiftly, out of reach. Just as I was about to give up and turn away, I saw something else lurking in the clouds below. The searchlight had illuminated another airship.

It was the SL–11, on its way to return home after dropping its bombs on the northern suburbs of London. Half an hour earlier, this airship had been the focus of most of the anti-aircraft guns in central London. They'd failed, but the volume of gunfire bursting around as SL–11 convinced its Captain to turn the giant ship around and head north.

I turned to face my enemy, the SL–11 vanished into a bank of clouds and twenty minutes passed. I contemplated returning home before my fuel ran out. The airship appeared again. Anti-aircraft guns were firing at it and searchlights occasionally caught the huge hole in their beam. I turned my BE2 to face the shadow. This time I would not let him slip away. I prepared to fire my machine gun. My plane rocked. I felt the heat from an explosion beneath me.

The anti-aircraft guns fired at the airship—the shells exploded at the height they guessed the target was flying. They had no idea my plane was up here also. Pilots didn't have radios to alert comrades below, but there was a procedure for these kinds of emergencies. I could fire off a flare, but this would also warn the airship crew that was stalking him. I pressed on and hoped my plane would not get hit.

I approached my target from below and swooped over to the front of the hull. As the vast shadow loomed over me, I fired my incendiary bullets into the great gas-filled body of the ship.

I flew nose down in the direction of the zeppelin. I saw shells bursting and night tracers flying around it. When I drew closer, I noticed that the anti-aircraft aim was aiming too low, and a good 800 feet behind. I flew below it from bow to stern and fired one full drum of ammunition along it. It seemed to have no effect.

I loaded a magazine into my machine gun—tricky process—trying to fly at the same time. The airship machine gun opened up on me. I weaved into the black night and then turned in for a second attempt. I emptied my entire ammunition drum again—and still, nothing happened.

After that run, I flew close to the crew control and saw the silhouettes of the men inside. They were aware I was attacking them. After all, they were involved in the bombing of the territory below. The roar of their own engines would have prevented them from hearing my tiny plane. I was getting angry. The incendiary bullets posed far more danger to the pilot firing them than the airship they were aimed at. But risking an attack from the guns of the Germans and my side, I flew in for a third time.

I got close behind it and concentrated one drum on one part. I barely finished the drum before I saw the part I fired at glow. When the third drum was fired, there were no searchlights on the zeppelin. No anti-aircraft was firing. I got out of the way of the following zeppelin. I was shaking with excitement and fired off two red flares and dropped a parachute flare.

Something remarkable happened inside the body the airship. The gas bag where I concentrated my fire ignited, lighting up the inside of the hull like a magic lantern.

The stern of the airship opened in an immense explosion and tossed my tiny plane like a paper dart in a gust of wind. The fire quickly spread along the entire body of the ship. I watched many of the crew throw themselves out of the zeppelin to avoid being burned to death.

I let off the rest of my flares, I was determined to let the anti-aircraft guns below know it was me that had downed the airship and not them. I turned my plane to return to the airbase. I noted the SL–II had already crashed into the ground. It was so bright; I could make out the shapes of houses all along the outer rim of Northeast London.

I proved it was possible to down these huge machines. Despite the early hour, all over London people rushed down the streets to sing and dance. The church bells rang, sirens wailed, ships' horns and motors tooted. The airships had caused such a terror for so long. But now we had gotten back at them.

Any other German airship crews most certainly would have seen the huge blaze lighting up the night sky in the far distance. The airships were not indestructible after all. The demise of the SL-II affected their performance because the raid on London that night was far from a success. While the airships dropped a huge number of bombs between them, only four people were killed and another twelve injured. Sixteen crewmen on board and SL-II lost their lives as the SL-II fell to earth behind the Plough Inn pub, next to the village of Cuffley, Hertfordshire.

The next day, the village was besieged by sightseers. The

country lanes nearby were clogged with cars, bicycles, carts, and pedestrians. The burned-out frame of tangled steel and wire, broken gondolas and smashed engines was a startling sight. On the side of the wreckage, a green tarp was laid out to hide the charred remains of crew that didn't leap to their deaths. Other bodies were found scattered over the countryside on SL-11's last, doomed flight.

My method of attack. A concentrated burst of incendiary fire at one concentrated spot was immediately passed on to all the fighter pilots that were likely to encounter a German airship. I was presented with the Victoria Cross, the highest award for bravery that can be given to members of the British armed forces.

But my fortunes declined, and I was shot down over Germany in occupied France only eight months later. I spent the rest of the war in a prison camp, where I was mistreated because it was known I shot down the SL–11. At the end of the war, I became one of the many millions of victims of a massive flu epidemic that swept through the world and died on New Year's Eve, 1918.

My victory had an impact far beyond the simple destruction of one airship. The swaggering confidence that airship crews had displayed in their mess halls and barracks were gone. Nights away from flying duty were haunted by dreams of burning airships. They were invulnerable no longer, like the gods of ancient Rome and Greece, casting death and destruction down from the skies. They were only flesh and blood. When death came, as it did with increasing regularity, the entire crew would perish.

It was from then on, that the zeppelin raids grew less frequent and more costly. From the spring of 1917, German bombers were sent over London instead. They were faster, flew higher and could defend themselves from fighter planes more effectively. Still, the Germans nursed high hopes for their magnificent airships.

By the end of the war, the latest model zeppelins were being prepared for a raid on New York. Luckily for the Americans, the war ended before such an attack was mounted.

THE BATTLE OF JUTLAND

In late May 1916, anyone who climbed the hills in the Scottish Orkney Islands could've seen through the mist and witnessed one of the most magnificent sites in naval history. This was the home of the grand British fleet. As far as the eye could see, there were rows of battleships, battle-cruisers, destroyers—and dozens of lesser vessels transporting messages and supplies between these deadly ships.

The ships were spaced at perfect intervals and exactly at the same angle to each other—a visible representation of the discipline and tradition of the British fighting forces. The power of the British Navy didn't end here with this collection of ships. There were other bases along the eastern coast of Scotland, each containing a formidable battle squadron of warships.

By the time the first world war started, Britain had the largest and most powerful fleet in the entire world. Our Island empire stretched from the Arctic to the Antarctic circles. Our warships protected the fleet of cargo ships that carried goods and raw materials to and from our colonies.

In wartime, our warships also prevented cargo ships from delivering supplies to our enemies. But most important of all, our fleet ensured that troops and supplies from England could safely sail across the channel to the Western Front in northern France.

Only Germany had a fleet powerful enough to threaten us. Kaiser Wilhelm II was the head of state of an up-and-coming superpower. He wanted to build a rival Navy to complement Germany's growing importance in the world. But the Kaiser's policy was a double-edged sword. His insistence on building a powerful navy had soured the previously good Anglo-German relations. It was one of the main reasons Britain decided to join France and Russia against Germany when war broke out.

At the start of the first world war, the battleship was considered the superweapon of the day. The largest and most heavily armed battleships were known as dreadnoughts—named after the HMS Dreadnought, the first of its kind launched in 1906.

The dreadnought weighed nearly 18 tons and packed a mighty punch with ten 12-inch guns. They could fire a shell that weighed over 1,400 pounds, nearly 13 miles. These guns were housed in pairs in large turrets. Usually at the front and rear of the ship. This type of weaponry gave the battleship its ferocious bite. Each of the gun turrets had a crew of around 70 men, split into teams who performed different tasks such as bringing up shells and propulsive charges from the ship's magazine. Then they loaded and accurately fired them. Working in a turret-like that is dangerous. If an enemy shell hits the turret, the entire mechanism would be engulfed in a massive explosion, killing everyone inside. The HMS Dreadnought overshadowed every other warship on the water.

Not only was it so powerfully armed, it was fast, and it had a thick metal protective covering as a shield. The ship carried a crew of over a thousand men and was nearly 700 feet from bow to stern. The arrival of the HMS Dreadnought started an expensive arms race between Germany and Britain. By the time the war broke out, we had built 28 ships and Germany had 16.

The revolutionary dreadnoughts were also joined by a new kind of warship, the battlecruiser, the first of their kind was called the HMS Invincible. It was launched in April 1907. Battlecruisers were as heavily armed as dreadnoughts but were smaller. They had eight 12-inch guns. They were faster than battleships and had a top speed of around twenty-five knots. Compared to a battleship twenty-one knots.

This speed was gained at the expense of having a lighter armor. When the war began in August 1914, a full-scale confrontation between the British and the German fleets seemed inevitable. Both countries built up their massive navies to face this upcoming fight. The German fleet was smaller than the British, but its ships were better designed. The Germans made very effective use of their U-boats; they sank countless cargo ships bound for Britain that the country was often in danger of starvation. The British never lost control of the sea. The Royal Navy blockaded German waters and prevented vital goods from entering. This caused great difficulty for the war industries of Germany and ensured that there was never enough food for her population.

Just six months into the war, a German battlecruiser was sunk in the North Sea, with great loss of life. For the first two years of the war, each Navy tested the strength of its opponents by pushing and probing and engaging in small-scale skirmishes. The carnage on the Western front continued with no visible benefit to either side. Pressure mounted on the German Navy's high command to force the British into a do or die battle that could tip the balance of the war in Germany's favor.

German high command decided to try and lure the British into the North Sea for a grand confrontation. If Germany succeeded, the war would be as good as won. With its fleet destroyed, we'd be completely helpless to prevent the German naval blockade around our coastal waters. Our food supplies will quickly run out and Britain would starve. Our troops and supplies would no longer be able to safely travel across the channel. The German plan was simple enough. They would send a bait battle cruiser squadron into the North Sea and would follow at a distance with the High Seas Fleet.

The British, it was hoped, would send out the wrong battle cruisers to intercept these German ships. They would almost certainly come from the base at Rosyth, nearest to the outgoing German ships. When the British were sighted on the horizon, the Germans would change course and lead the enemy back to the main battle fleet. Where they'd be outnumbered and destroyed.

The plan also assumed that the main British naval force —called the Grand Fleet—would take to the sea as well, from more northerly of the base. Here the Germans placed U-boats to pick them off as they sailed to intercept. The Germans intended to use zeppelins to keep watch on the British Navy and radio information on the movements of her ships.

But just like many simple plans, there were unforeseen problems.

On May 31st, 1916, the Germans put their plan in motion.

From bases on the northern coast to Germany, the High Seas Fleet took to sea. The Germans had five battlecruisers and another thirty-five smaller ships to trying to lure the British Navy into a battle. Another German fleet followed closely behind with sixty more battleships, battlecruisers, destroyers, and cruisers. By 1 o'clock that afternoon, two German Squadrons were out in the North Sea over 50 miles apart.

As they hoped, the German squadron was soon sighted by British reconnaissance ships that patrolled the coast of Germany. British intelligence picked up and decoded German radio signals, which indicated that there was a buildup of German ships in the North Sea. The British immediately ordered their battle cruiser squadron under Adm. Beatty to take to sea. Unknown to the Germans, the British were already at sea with the Grand Fleet, patrolling an area of the North Sea known as the long 40s a hundred and ten miles east of Aberdeen. The Grand Fleet was ordered to head south and follow Adm. Beatty. Between them, the British had a hundred and forty-nine ships under their command.

This set the stage for an epic battle. To this day, no greater naval battle has ever taken place. The opposing admirals perched high in their respective command posts on the decks of their ships. They began the game that was a strange combination of chess and hide and go seek. At stake were the lives of over 100,000 sailors and the fate of nearly 250 ships and quite possibly the outcome of the first world war. The British were hoping for a victory to match Trafalgar. (Wherein 1805 the Royal Navy under Adm. Nelson destroyed the French and Spanish fleets and gained undisputed control of the sea for the next century.)

Right from the start, the German plan had problems.

The U-boats stationed outside the bases on the Scottish coast failed to attack the British ships as they emerged to patrol the North Sea. Due to a technical problem, the wireless orders permitting them to engage their enemy was never received. The Germans' use of zeppelins as reconnaissance aircraft was also a failure, due to poor visibility and bad weather. The zeppelins could see nothing through the cloud and foggy haze. This was a major setback. In 1916, naval guns and ships were more sophisticated and powerful than those used by Adm. Nelson in Trafalgar. Still, the communication and detection technology was much the same. The Germans might've had guns that could fire a heavy shell over 14 miles, but they still looked for their enemy with the telescope and the naked eye.

Also, due to the danger of wireless communications being intercepted by the enemy in battle, they still preferred to communicate with their ships using signal flags.

Earlier that afternoon, neither navy knew the size of the enemy fleet that was fast approaching. We thought the German squadron was at sea, and the Germans had no idea they were about to face the entire British Grand Fleet.

Adm. Beatty's fleet first sighted the German ships at around 2 o'clock when they were 75 miles off the Danish coast. This started in an epic naval confrontation that would forever be known as the battle of Jutland.

The first shots fired off 15 minutes later, between small scouting ships that sailed ahead of the main fleets. It was a hazy day. The sun hid behind the German ships giving them a better view of the approaching enemy. We sailed forward to engage the German forces. By then, it was already 3:30. We knew the British Grand Fleet was coming up behind us, and we'd be on our own for several hours.

The Germans knew they had to lure Adm. Betty's ships into the jaws of the High Seas Fleet behind them. As they had done in the days of Adm. Nelson in Trafalgar. Both fleets sailed in line, one after the other, in tight formation.

At 4 o'clock, the battlecruisers began to fire at each other. The odds seemed to be on our side. We had six battlecruisers, the Germans only five. The firing was so constant that each squadron navigated its way through the thick forest of towering shell splashes. In the no man's land between the fleet, a small sailboat sat motionless. Its sails hung limp as deadly shells whistled and screamed over the heads of the hapless sailors on board.

The superiority of the German guns and ships were obvious. Only twelve minutes into the fighting, one of our battlecruisers became the first major casualty of the day. The Germans landed three shells on her simultaneously. The HMS Indefatigable disappeared into a vast cloud of black smoke, twice the height of her mast. She fell out of line as two more shells exploded on her deck. Something terrible was happening, I watched as the searing flames gnawed at her ammunition. Thirty seconds after the second shells hit, the entire ship exploded, sending huge fragments of metal high into the air.

She rolled over and sank a moment later.

Several other British ships were hit, including Adm. Beatty's own battle cruiser, The HMS Lion. A shell exploded on the central turret and blew half the roof into the air, killing the entire gun crew. The guns roared and shells whistled as they approached, it was enough to distract anyone from what was happening around them. We barely noticed the loss of HMS Indefatigable. We had enough troubles of our own. Six more shells from the Germans hit our ship within four minutes of each other, and fires raged on deck and below. Thirty minutes later, another explosion caused by the slow-burning fires shot up as high as the masthead. But still, we survived to fight on.

Other British ships in the fighting had to contend with similar problems. In less than an hour, the battlecruiser Queen Mary blew up, breaking in half and sinking in less than two minutes. The ammunition supplies exploded. The huge gun turrets were blown 100 feet into the air. Only eight men survived from the entire ship.

I watched the Queen Mary sink, and I knew deep down in my bones, I had to get away. I dove into the freezing, oily water and swam as fast as I could away from the ship. A minute later, there was a huge explosion, and chunks of metal filled the air around me. I dove deep beneath the waves to avoid the flying fragments. I reached the surface and gasped for breath. I was drug under the water again from the suction of the ship as it sank.

Underneath the water, I felt helpless and resigned to my own fate. But something made me strike out for the surface. Just as I felt I was about to lose consciousness, I broke through the waves. I saw a piece of floating debris and wrapped my wrist around the rope trailing from it before I lost consciousness. I was eventually rescued, but not before an earlier ship picked up other survivors and left me for dead.

Afterward, Adm. Beatty commented on the destruction of the Queen Mary. In the pretentious manner of the British upper class at war, he said:

> *"There seems to be something wrong with our bloody ships today."*

There was something wrong with the British ships. They were poorly designed. German warships had solid bulkheads passable by going to the upper deck and then down into the next section. British ships had bulkheads with doors that permitted passage between them. This was far more convenient, but a serious weakness when a massive explosion ripped through the ship. The British also had a much more careless attitude about their ammunition.

The Germans kept their ammunition and shells locked away and blast-proof containers until they were ready to be fired. While British gunners piled the shells next to the guns. This made it far easier to accidentally set off if the ship was hit.

Just moments after the Queen Mary sank, the German High Seas Fleet was spotted on the horizon, steaming toward us to join the battlecruiser squadron. The rest of our British Grand Fleet was still a good 12 miles away. Now was time to test Adm. Betty's composure to the limit. He faced the full might of the German Navy and had already lost two battleship cruisers. Adm. Beatty gave the signal for a full hundred-and eighty-degree turn.

The German plan was to entice the British into the jaws of their full might. The German ships pursued. Adm. Beatty had lured them into the mass firepower of the British Grand Fleet. Just after 5 o'clock, the Germans had come close enough to Beatty's retreating ships to begin attacking the stragglers. But an hour later, the British Grand Fleet of twenty-four battleships steamed over the horizon.

No matter how good the German ships were, they were heavily outnumbered. The Germans were in serious trouble, and they sent the order to retreat North. Were the Germans trying to lead us into a trap, hoping that the British would blunder into a minefield or right into the arms of waiting submarines? There was too much at stake. The British decided not to follow. Instead, they ordered their ships South hoping to again make contact with the German fleet.

Another British ship, the HMS invincible, became the third major victim of the day. A shell hit one of her turrets, causing a huge explosion which broke the ship in two. Only six men survived on the crew of over a thousand. For a while, the bow and stern of this huge battlecruiser stood motionless in the water; it looks like two church spires in a sunken village. Then, the stern sunk to the bottom of the sea. The bow stayed upright until almost the next day when it also sank. Those trapped inside must've spent an agonizing night, wondering what on earth was happening to them in their topsy-turvy world. They surely expected to be swallowed by the sea when the ship went vertical in the water. Their inevitable death would be drawn out for a few more miserable hours.

As the evening wore on, the British intuition that the German ships would head south proved correct. Just after 7 o'clock, the two fleets sighted each other again. The Germans made several moves to try and gain an advantage over the British fleet. Both sides followed a tactic known as crossing the T. This idea was to line up your fleet of warships at a right angle to your opponents, as they approached you in a straight line. So, your fleet made the top of the T and the enemy fleet made the descending stroke. That way, the captain could fire all guns aboard ships on both the bow and the stern, while the enemy would only be able to use his front guns.

But the Germans failed and disastrously found their ships scattered at an angle to the approaching British fleet. Worse, the sun was now behind the British and it was only possible to see them by the flash of their guns. At this point in the battle, it was the British shells that were falling with greater accuracy and the German ships were faltering.

It was at precisely this moment the Germans made the most ruthless decision of the day. To avoid their entire fleet being reduced to wreckage by the much larger British force, the Germans took four of their battlecruisers and sailed straight at the British fleet. Their signal read, battlecruisers at the enemy. Give it everything. There is a cruel logic to this decision. The Germans used their older and less powerful warships. This action has become known as the death ride. The Germans intended the British fleet to concentrate their fire on this attacking squadron while allowing the rest of the High Seas Fleet to turn around and escape.

These four German ships had been in the thick of action since the battle began. They'd all sustained serious damage. As they headed out into the fading light, each ship's captain was convinced he would not live to see the coming night. But in warfare, nothing is predictable. Ahead of them, the British Grand Fleet stretched in a curve as far as they could see. Every one of these British ships fired at the approaching German battlecruisers. The first battlecruiser suffered direct hits on its rear turrets, exploding with horrific consequences for those inside. Due to good design, the rest of the ship survived. The other German battlecruisers suffered similar blows. Although they took many hits from British shells, the ships were not blown to pieces.

The German commander was brave, but he had no intention of committing suicide. Once he was sure the rest of the German fleet had escaped, he turned his ships away to rejoin the rear of the departing squadron. The British became suspicious. Rather than following the German ships directly, they decided to head south and raced to catch them in more of an indirect route. As the sun sank on the horizon, the German squadron was caught again by the British. This time they weren't so lucky. One German battlecruiser sustained more damage and sank later that night. While the other three battlecruisers were severely damaged.

In the dark, the opposing navies exchanged fire, but the main action was over. Another German battleship was sunk. Torpedoes from British destroyers caught her close to home, and all 866 men on board were killed.

Dawn broke around 3 o'clock in the morning on June 1. The British hoped to resume contact with the German fleet at first light, but the lookouts strained their eyes over an empty sea. The German ships were in sight of their home-port. This battle was over.

The two greatest navies in the world took part in one great sea battle of the First World War. It was also to be the last great sea battle in history. Battleships would never again meet in such numbers. As the century wore on, there would be Naval weapons even deadlier than the great ones that the battleships carried–submarines, dive bombers, etc. The technological advances made battleships too vulnerable to be useful weapons.

The German gamble failed. The events of the day show that they had every right to be confident. Germany's ships were better than Britain's and they proved this by sinking more of the enemy's fleet. The British had lost 14 ships and over 6,000 men. The Germans lost 11 ships and over 1500 men. The day after the battle, it looked like a German victory.

But in the end, the might of the Royal Navy had prevailed again. We still controlled the sea. Like the other grand battles of 1916 at Verdun and the Somme, this clash of huge opposing forces had taken place, and nothing changed. The British hadn't lost the war in an afternoon after all. We hadn't won it either, but we ensured that Germany would not win it.

After the battle, the tactics employed by the British were discussed and dissected in clinical detail. The communication between British ships had been abysmal and Adm. Beatty was criticized for not attacking the German fleet with more enthusiasm. In hindsight, the British still came out of it in a much better position than the Germans. It only took us a day to recover from the battle, before we were able to announce that our fleet was once again ready for whatever threat it might face.

The German High Seas Fleet never put to sea again.

The outcome of the battle of Jutland had far-reaching consequences. As the High Seas Fleet proved unable to undermine British control of the seas, the German high command decided to adopt the policy of unrestricted U-boat warfare instead. Their submarines were given permission to attack any ship, including neutral ones, that came into British waters.

This change of tactics led to the sinking of American ships, which was one of the main reasons the US entered the war against Germany—a move that sealed her fate.

The German High Seas Fleet remained in port for the rest of the war. Boredom and poor rations led to mutinies at the end of the war, and ultimately revolutionary insurrection. After the armistice of November 1918, the fleet was ordered to sea, while peace terms were discussed in Paris.

Just before the peace treaty was signed in the summer of 1919, it was ordered that the High Seas Fleet would be split up, and it ships given to the victorious nations. But this was too much to bear for the skeleton crews of the German sailors left aboard the ships. They scuttled and deliberately sank their Navy. Most of these vast, magnificent warships were eventually raised from the sea bottom and towed away for scrap.

But some remain to this day and are a source of fascination for divers.

OBLIVION AT THE SOMME

My journey began in the first few days following the outbreak of war. Most soldiers that took part in this great battle were volunteers who joined up at the beginning. We were dubbed Kitchener's Army after the British war secretary, Lord Kitchener, who was on recruitment posters asking for volunteers all over Britain.

Millions of men flocked to join. We were enticed by the promise that we could serve alongside our friends in what became known as the *PALs* battalions. This was a great idea in theory. Soldiers within the regiment would be made up of men from the same village, town, or workplace. We trained and worked together, and when the time came, we fought together.

I was from a smoky, industrial town in Lancashire. We provided a *PALs* battalion for the East Lancashire Regiment. When the war broke out, the town hit hard times. There was a strike at the local textile machinery factory and at the cotton mill. They laid off over 500 men. Most men rushed to join up for the benefit of a soldier's pay instead of any patriotic motive. The pay was twice what we got in the factory.

Those not tempted by financial gain faced more subtle pressures. I remember one recruitment poster that said:

> *"Will you fight for your king and country, or will you*
> *cower in the safety your fathers and brothers struggled to*
> *maintain?"*

Another recruitment poster carried a much more personal message; it was a young man being shamed by his girlfriend's father. It said:

> *"If you're old enough to walk out with my daughter,*
> *you're old enough to fight for her and your country."*

Whatever other reasons we had for joining, many men did so just for patriotism—it was an unquestionable feeling of duty and love for country. Lancashire was very poor, and a good number of those who flocked to enlist were small and malnourished. Many men failed their medical examination and were rejected as recruits. Much to their humiliation and disappointment after the outcry in the region, the British Army dropped the standards.

Instead of requiring recruits to be at least 18 and over 5'6" tall with a chest measurement of 35 inches, the rules were relaxed to just 5'3" tall and a 34-inch measurement in the chest. Age was never a problem; it was always easy enough for 16-year-old to pass as a soldier, and this was rarely checked.

When it was time to go, we lined up in the market square and marched down to the grimy granite railway station—watched by the whole town. We stood on the overcrowded platforms and waited for the steam train that would whisk us away from our familiar world. I look back now and see photographs of myself and other men smiling for the camera. The truth is, we had no idea what we were getting ourselves into.

As 1915 ended, the British and French military commands became convinced that the way to end the war would be through one big push. It was to be a massive attack on a broad front that would be enough to finally break through the German lines and form a gap for the cavalry to rush through. This tactic would reinstate a war of movement instead of the stalemate of the trenches.

The spot chosen for this big push was the Somme, a chalky part of northern France near the Belgian border named after the river that ran through it. There was no strategic value to the Somme. The allies wanted to take it because it was the area of the Western Front where the British and French lines met. It was the most convenient spot for a combined attack

As 1916 began, the Germans had their own plans. They intended to wear down the French army by a constant attack. The Germans launched a battle of attrition on the French fortress of Verdun. It started in February 1916 and succeeded all too well, though at a terrible cost to their army.

The French army never recovered from the fighting at Verdun. It was in no position to offer more than token support to us when their own big push began in the summer.

Our commander, British Field Marshal Haig, commanded the British troops in that section of the front, and he began the final plan for the battle of the Somme. Haig had overall command of the armies which numbered 58 divisions. Most of these men were Kitchener's Army recruits that joined in 1914. We were trained and ready to fight and we were keen to show what we could do.

From right from the start, there was something unimaginative about Haig's tactics. Field Marshall Haig was convinced God had helped him with his battle plans. The date for our opening attack was July 1, at 7:30 in the morning, after a five-day bombardment by over a thousand artillery guns. It was way too obvious to the enemy. The five-day bombardment indicated an attack was imminent as clearly as if you wrote it with smoke from a biplane. Those like me who'd rushed to join up, with pure enthusiasm for the war, were about to find out the true nature of 20th-century warfare.

In the evening before the attack, we were taken to the frontline trenches. We marched past open mass graves, freshly dug in anticipation of the heavy casualties to come.

I was closer to the enemy than I'd ever been, and I tried to settle in my uncomfortable position and ready myself for the next morning. Sleep during the artillery bombardment was impossible.

On the day before the offensive, the commanding officers briefed us on the task ahead. We were told that the trenches we were going to attack would be undefended—the five-day bombardment would see to that and would also cut the barbed wire in front of the German trenches to pieces. The generals were so confident that we'd have no problems taking the German frontline, troops were sent to battle with over 60 pounds of equipment. It was like carrying two heavy suitcases into battle. They expected us to occupy the German front lines and repel any counterattacks.

The Somme was not a good place to launch an attack. The main reason for its location—the joining point of the British and French front lines—had been reduced to a minor consideration after Verdun. Only five French divisions were going to take part in this battle, while we had fourteen British ones. All along the front, the Germans occupied the higher ground. We had to advance uphill.

The chalky ground made it much easier for the Germans to dig in. They were 40 feet underground and had constructed heavily fortified positions that were nearly immune to the five-day bombardment. The five days of shelling wasn't as impressive as it sounded. The over one million shells fired were produced in haste and the quality control had been nonexistent. Most of the shells were duds and never exploded.

The ones that did explode churned up the ground in front of the German trenches and made it more difficult to pass through in our attack. When the artillery bombardment ended at 7:30 in the morning, several huge explosions rocked the German trenches. These explosives were placed in mines dug at intervals under German positions along 18 miles of the front designated for the attack.

After this mountainous explosion of the earth, a strange silence settled over the battlefield. The constant roar of the last five days seemed unnatural. I imagined the German soldiers knew immediately that something was about to happen. They quickly emerged from their bunkers and set up their machine guns.

All along the battlefront, whistles blew. It was the signal to attack. We climbed up wooden ladders placed along the outer edge of the front-line trenches. We arranged ourselves into neat lines that we learned to form in training and marched into No Man's Land in successive waves.

Some of us had tin discs on our backs to glint in the sun. The idea was to show the artillery where we were so we wouldn't get hit by our own shells that fell short. It was a bright summer morning and so hot that we felt the heat of the sun on the backs of our necks. It was Field Marshal Haig's plan of action that called for the soldiers to advance in straight lines to a precise timetable. They decided against sending advance parties to check if the razor wire had been destroyed. The idea was that we were so inexperienced and incapable of following anything but the simplest plan. There was to be no flexibility or initiative, just momentum. We were a vast, sprawling tide of men meant to sweep the Germans from their positions.

I was in the first wave as we advanced.

As we approached the German lines, I saw to my horror that the wire had not been destroyed at all. Our artillery shells had just blown the barbed wire into the air and then it settled back down again where it had previously been. There were some gaps in the wire, but we soon learned that these were deliberately left by the Germans to herd us into killing zones, where they'd concentrate their machine-gun fire on us.

According to the British military command, any Germans who survived the bombardment were supposed to become disoriented and overwhelmed by the sheer size of the force arrayed against them. But instead, they just got on with the grisly business of butchering us. They set up machine guns that fired 600 bullets a minute and mowed us down like we were corn before the scythe. A captain in the eighth battalion gave the signal to attack by climbing onto the rim of his trench. He kicked a football into the direction of the enemy lines. I'm sure he was trying to allay the fears of his men with a show of bravado, but he was instantly killed shot through the head and undermined the effect he tried to create.

I continued walking forward in a glassy delirium. All

around me, men fell to the ground. Some gently, others rolling and screaming. I pressed on unscathed as my friends and comrades were shot to pieces. Three other waves came up behind me and suffered the same fate. I looked along the line and realized there were only a few of us left.

Following the plan, our attack went on all morning, with four waves of men going out to face the same grim fate. The British Army was probably the most rigid and inflexible fighting force of the war. The junior officers in the heat of battle were expected to follow their orders to the letter. At any cost. Even If they found themselves in impossible circumstances.

The communications between the officers at the front and the generals at the rear were poor. They were dependent on telephone lines, which were broken by shell fire and runners to carry messages from the front to the rear, who were often killed. The officers were briefed to order soldiers to go forward at any cost, and they did despite the obvious futility. Field Marshal Haig might as well of ordered us to march off a cliff.

By the early afternoon, the news of our slaughter trickled back and Army headquarters and further attacks for that day were called off. The casualty figures were the worst for any single day in the history of the British Army. And the worst for any day, in any army, in the entire war.

Back at the casualty clearing stations in the rear, I watched and then returned from No Man's Land, milling around in confusion, searching for a familiar face. We had our roll call ritual, which established who had returned from the attack and who hadn't. So many of my friends that were missing, they must've been killed or wounded. All those bullets, all those bullets and not one with my name on it. I felt like I was the luckiest man in the world.

Of the hundred and twenty thousand men who took part in the first mornings fighting, half were casualties. There were over 20,000 men killed, and another 40,000 men wounded. That night, there was a slow trickle of men that'd been injured in No Man's Land. They spent the day hiding in shell craters, suffering through the hot sun and returning to their trenches under cover of darkness.

I found out later that the British press reported the attack and that the battle was a great victory. They described the disaster as a good day for England. The paper read:

"A slow, continuous and methodical push, sparing in lives."

I'm sure these reports were to reassure anxious families at home, but for other soldiers who took part in this attack and me, I was angry. There were some battalions who came through with only a few casualties. But there were others that had suffered terribly.

Another battalion started the day with 24 officers and 650 men. At roll call that evening, only a single officer and 50 men remained. The Lancashire PALs were among the first to attack the German line that morning and lost 584 men out of 720—killed, wounded or vanished—in the first half-hour of the battle. Despite the complete lack of any reliable news from the front, our families in Lancashire begin to suspect something terrible happened to us. The regular flow of letters from France also stopped.

A week after the battle started, a train full of wounded soldiers from the Somme briefly stopped at Lancashire station on the way to an Army hospital further north. A man in the train called out to a group of women on the platform. He was told that the Lancashire *PALs* had been wiped out.

The news spread quickly and created an awful atmosphere, like dull, heavy air before a thunderstorm and hung over the town. Letters from wounded men ensuring their families that they were still alive, began to trickle in. The letters came in such numbers, and it was obvious that something big had happened. Those who hadn't received a letter were left in a terrible limbo—should they hope for the best or fear the worst?

There is something even worse about the battle at the Somme and the 60,000 casualties in a single morning. Despite the losses, Field Marshal Haig remained convinced that his failure was in not sending enough men. He thought the big push wasn't big enough. For the next five months, the volunteers of Kitchener's Army were sent into a hideous grinding machine to be destroyed in the thousands. Caught in barbed wire and riddled by machine-gun bullets.

There were a few successes through the carnage. A night attack on July 4th caught the Germans by surprise, five miles of the front-line and the German trenches were over-run. The next morning, this breakthrough was followed up by a cavalry charge—the standard tactic used in 19th-century warfare—when the enemy's front line was pierced. The cavalrymen didn't look quite as dashing as they once did. The red jackets had been traded for a dull khaki. The bugle still blew, and lances glittered in the hot summer sun. Like all cavalry charges, it was a magnificent sight. Until it ended in a hail of machine-gun bullets, flailing hooves and twitching bodies.

Even the Australian troops made it to the Western Front and fought with great courage. Three weeks into the battle they captured a local village but paid a terrible price for the victory. So many men were killed, that an Australian soldier described it to me as:

*"The bloodiest, heaviest, rottenest stunt that ever
Australians were caught up in."*

On September 15, 1916, tanks were employed for the first time in history. We pinned our hopes on these new weapons, machine gun destroyers as they were called at the time. For a German machine gunner in his trench, there was nothing as terrifying as facing a huge tank. Metal tracks clanking and grinding, lumbering slowly forward to crush through the defense of the barbed wire, bullets bouncing off its heavy steel flank. The tank would eventually prove to be one of the most effective weapons of the century—but not at the Battle of the Somme. Most broke down before they could even reach the front line.

After 140 days, when the battle finally halted in November 1916, over a million men had been killed or wounded. In all, there were over four hundred thousand British casualties, two hundred thousand French and a half a million German. The defenders were mostly the soldiers of the German 2nd Army. They suffered so many casualties because of their own generals. Giving orders that ground gained by the British or French had to be recaptured at any cost. The German high command also forbid the voluntary evacuation of trenches. They were ordered to stand firm and told they would have to carve their out way over heaps of corpses.

Our troops were mowed down in the thousands attacking front-line German trenches. The British soldiers exacted an act of grim revenge, as our enemy exposed themselves to similar carnage to win back lost ground. I remember thinking, you've given it to us, now it's our turn. Our machine gunners had a great time mowing down the German soldiers that rushed blindly into our bullets. Any positive military advantage from this destruction was almost unnoticeable.

In some areas along the 18-mile front, the front line been redrawn by five miles here and there, but, like other battles the first World War, death on such an industrial scale did not serve any useful purpose. Soldiers in the British Army would never again show such misplaced enthusiasm for battle. From then on, ordinary soldiers referred to the campaign on the Somme with a heartfelt and bitter loathing. To this day, the horror and carnage of the early hours of that Saturday morning still shocks me as I think about the war.

For those who took part in it and survived, it would be the defining moment of their lives. I still remember how the first day merged into the second. When I held grimly onto a battered trench and watched each of my fellow soldiers grow old through the day-long storm of the shelling. For hours we prayed, sweat, and swore as we worked on the heaps of chalk and mangled bodies.

At dawn the next morning, we were back in the green wood. I found myself leaning on my rifle and staring stupidly at the filthy exhausted men sleeping around me.

It didn't occur to me to lie down until someone pushed me into a bed of ferns. There were flowers among the ferns, and one of my last thoughts was if there could still be flowers in the world.

MUTINY ON THE WESTERN FRONT

The word mutiny conjures up images of drunken violence and a descent into anarchy. It's a word that would make an officer's blood run cold. Without order and obedience, one man cannot tell another man to carry out actions that will result in death and injury. Mutiny renders an army ineffective faster than a curtain of machine-gun fire or even an artillery barrage. It can lead to an utter defeat in a matter of days, so generally, they punished it with great severity.

In ancient Rome, mutinous Army legions that returned to military discipline were subject to decimation. One man in 10 was plucked from the ranks and executed publicly. Who could ever guess, this ancient, barbaric remedy would be employed again in the 20th century, to restore order to the French Army.

The French mutinies of 1917 had their roots in the German army's decision to fight the war by taking French lives rather than French territory. In February 1916, the Germans chose the French fortress of Verdun to do exactly this. In a horrible 10-month battle, the French and Germans fought for possession of the stronghold. Much of the fighting took place in dank, concrete forts washed with blood and immersed in the stark terror of men in hand-to-hand combat.

When the battle ended in December of that year, over 350,000 French soldiers and 330,000 German soldiers had been killed or injured.

There was nothing to show for the slaughter.

No territory had been won or lost. Each side lost an equal number of troops. The Germans changed their high leadership and tactics, but by then, their strategy of bleeding the French army white had more of an effect then they'd realized.

The French people were immensely proud of their army successes in defending Verdun. The soldiers battle cry: they shall not pass, became the slogan of national self-esteem. French generals became national heroes. But after the battle for Verdun, many French soldiers felt that they had nothing left to give.

Another major French offensive was planned in the early spring of 1917. The French high command promised their troops a quick victory at Chemin des

Dames, down on the river Aisne. The French soldiers were told that this would be the battle to win the war. Morale was high, especially when French soldiers were told that they'd be time trying a new tactic to save their lives. They'd head over the German trenches, under the protection of the creeping barrage, a hail of shells which would fall in front of them, advancing like a protective wall of fire.

Tanks would be used, a new type of weapon which promised to crush the barb wire defense and destroy the deadly machine gun nest, which swept away scores of men with a single burst of fire.

A million men took part in the attack on April 16. It failed. It was another senseless slaughter. The tanks broke down and the artillery bombardment failed to destroy enemy strong points. The weather didn't help either and French soldiers had to advance in the driving rain. After 10 days, over 30,000 men had been killed, with over 20,000 missing, almost certainly dead. Another 90,000 men had been wounded. But still, the attacks continued.

Not all the soldiers believed the French generals promises of an easy victory in a decisive breakthrough. Many companies of men, including my own, marched to the front bleating like sheep. We believe that we were lambs led to the slaughter. It was a warning sign that was ignored. Chemin des Dames became the place where the morale of the French army finally collapsed.

The first mutiny was with the 2nd Battalion of the 18th infantry Regiment. Out of 600 men, only 200 had survived the offensive. After a brief respite behind the French front lines, they were once again ordered back to the trenches. It was the early evening of April 29, 1917. Many of the men were drunk on cheap red wine that was always supplied free to the French troops. Almost all men refused to return and gathered in large groups shouting down to the war. But, by early next morning, the men sobered up and marched back to the front line.

As we marched, the officers of the Battalion decided this insurrection should be immediately punished. At random, a dozen men were pulled out from our ranks and charged with mutiny. They shot five of them. Another had an amazing escape. As he was being led to the firing squad by a group of guards, a German artillery bombardment fell around them. He ran into the nearby woods and was never seen again.

A few days later, another mutiny broke out. This was far more serious and involved the entire 2nd division. Thousands of men—almost all drunk—refused to carry weapons and return to the trenches. When the drink wore off, most of the men gave in and marched to the front. The few who refused to go were quickly arrested, and no one else in the division was singled out for punishment.

This was only the beginning. In early May, this drunken rebellion spread throughout the Army. It was an odd sort of mutiny. There were no reports of officers being attacked or killed and no political demands. When officers spoke to the man elected by their comrades to represent them. They were told the soldiers would continue to defend their trenches. But they would no longer take part in the attacks against the Germans.

While large-scale mutiny swept the ranks of the French army, extraordinary events took place in Russia. A similar widespread mutiny led to the overthrow of the czarist government, deeply alarming the other allies. The French authorities were lucky there were no equivalents of Lenin and Trotsky among their troops. If there had been, the history of France, over the course of the 20th century might've been very different. The French rebellion had no obvious leaders; it wasn't being directed by anyone. Despite this, the need to spread so fast that by June, 54 divisions over half of the entire French army in the Western front were affected. Over 30,000 men just left the frontline posts and tried to walk home.

The causes of mutiny were straightforward. The ordinary French soldier had lost faith in his generals. He wasn't prepared to lay down his life for a way of fighting that he no longer believed in. There were other causes, and these are serious enough to make anyone wonder why the mutiny had not happened before.

Compared to the British, French soldiers had to put up with harsher conditions in military discipline. Their pay was awful. The food they had to eat was often cold and the poor quality—an especially troubling state of affairs for such a nation of gourmets. The British Army made a great effort to keep its soldiers supplied with hot food of reasonable quality. British soldiers from the other side of the channel also spent more time away from the trenches and with their families, than French soldiers.

This was especially painful for the French, as many were fighting less than a day's train journey away from their homes. But they were rarely offered leave. All sides suffered horrendous casualties, of the allies; the French lost the most men. One in four Frenchmen between the ages of 18 and 30 would die in the war. Over a million and a half in all. With millions more wounded and maimed for life.

In the French high command, the mutiny caused a panic. France had already suffered so much. So many men had been sacrificed to keep the German army from overrunning our country. How awful would it be if the French lost the war because its soldiers gave up and went home. For these reasons, the French high command chose to address their soldiers' complaints rather than simply suppress the revolt with brutality.

The French leadership had three significant problems.

First, they had to take immediate steps to introduce reforms to make life more bearable for their men. Most of whom were conscripts fighting for the duration of the war, rather than career soldiers.

Second, to uphold this plan, the Army had to punish

those responsible. A difficult task because the mutiny really did lack ringleaders.

Third, and most important of all, they had to keep the mutiny secret from the Germans. If they knew what was going on, they could break through the French lines and be in Paris within a week. Then the war would be lost for sure.

Several older generals were replaced. The quality of food fed to front-line troops was drastically improved. A system of home leave was introduced, and rest camps behind the front lines were made more habitable. The French high command made it clear to the junior officers and NCOs that ordinary soldiers' lives would not be thrown away in useless offensives.

Punishment for the mutiny was still random and unfair. In early June, a battalion of 700 men marched back to the front and disappeared into the forest at the side of the road. Earlier that day, word spread to the troops that there was a massive cave in which they all could hide. The commander showing remarkable bravery went into the cave and talked to the mutineers. He told them to return to the front by daybreak, or they'd all be slaughtered. The men came out. Once they were back under the Army command, 20 were pulled from the ranks and shot.

The French commander neglected to mention that this would happen. But, in other divisions, once order had been restored, the momentary mutiny was quickly forgotten and no one was punished.

In all, over 24,000 men were arrested and put before military courts. Of these, 551 were judged to be leaders of the revolt and sentenced to death. But only 40 were shot. The rest were sent to the penal colony of French Guiana—a miserable fate for conscripted soldiers who fought bravely until they could take no more. The executed were shot in front of their comrades, who then marched past the dead men.

Other French soldiers were shot at random and without trial, but the number of those deaths is difficult to estimate. The mutiny was dealt with sensitively. But underneath the concern, there was an iron fist, determined that such widespread disobedience would never be allowed to happen again.

Among the rebellious divisions was a regiment of Russian soldiers, sent to the Western Front as a goodwill gesture by the ailing czarist regime before they were overthrown. Those soldiers had endured worse conditions and even more incompetent leadership the French and British allies. They were ready to follow the example of their rebellious French comrades' mutiny. Their fate was pitiful. The French command had to deal with their own soldiers with some leniency. There were too many to punish. A harsh discipline might've provoked a worse rebellion and even possibly a revolution. The Russians were expendable. The regiment was surrounded and blown to pieces by the French artillery.

The mutiny lasted for six weeks. The French army escaped a crushing defeat by the skin of their teeth. But the soldiers sent a clear message to their generals. From now on, there would be no more mass attacks. French soldiers would only take part in small-scale assaults on the German lines. This put the horrific bloodletting of the previous three years to an end. For the rest of the war, the lion share of the fighting against the Central Powers would be left to Britain and the fresh, enthusiastic American troops. The United States had entered the war just in time to save the allies from inevitable defeat.

Behind the front lines, the government reacted by tightening censorship in French newspapers and imprisoning those who campaigned for an end to the war. These days, such people would be called peace campaigners. In 1917, they were called into war agitators.

Even now, the mutiny is a shameful and touchy subject in France. On its 80th anniversary in 1997, the French Prime Minister suggested the mutineers needed to be understood and forgiven. This was denounced harshly by the then French Pres. Jacques Chirac. The act of expressing sympathy for those war-weary men was still considered an outrage.

But now, most people agree that the mutineers deserve pity rather than condemnation.

They were simply men who got lost in a hell of fire and blood.

BELLEAU WOOD NIGHTMARE

The year before we entered the war, the United States had a small army of barely 100,000 men. The President, Woodrow Wilson, had mixed feelings about committing our country to the conflict. Many American citizens were European immigrants that had fled the New World, partly to avoid wars just like this. Not to mention, a sizable proportion of America's immigrants were from Germany. This complicated any decision about which side to support.

In January 1917, German military commanders decided to allow their U-boats to sink any ship found in British waters. This caused the destruction of American cargo ships and the occasional passenger liner. This shifted public opinion from wary neutrality to a completely anti-German outlook.

President Wilson guessed the time was right. So, on April 17, the United States finally joined the war on the side of the allies. Once we joined the conflict, we set out to prove ourselves to the world.

We were an enthusiastic, prosperous and upcoming nation. After the war in 1918, we had over four million US citizens in the armed forces and three and a half million of them had been transported over to Europe. They came in packed like sardines vis ocean liners hurriedly transformed into troop ships.

We slept in bunk beds made of steel and wire stacked four high on top of each other. The journey was so uncomfortable that many soldiers, including me, found the trenches more comfortable.

The Germans knew that America joining the Allies would make their own victory almost impossible. But in 1917, the war was going Germany's way, Russia was in the throes of revolution and desperate to make peace and end the fighting on the Eastern Front.

Germany wanted to annihilate the sapped French and British soldiers with the full force of their army. At the beginning of 1918, American troops ships with newly trained soldiers began to arrive in France. But still, at that time, there were only a few thousand American troops in Europe.

It was going to take time to raise and prepare a fighting force, almost from scratch, and then to transport the huge numbers of men across the Atlantic. The German generals knew that to win the war in the West, they would have to strike hard and fast before the Americans came in overwhelming numbers. So, at the end of March, the Germans launched a carefully planned attack, known as the Ludendorff offensive.

The German troops used a new tactic and smashed through the Allied front lines. They employed surprise attacks to discover weak spots and by using overwhelming strength when they found them.

All spring, the German troops made a series of remarkable advances, which caused panic in the British Empire and among the French forces. In April, the British commander in chief, Field Marshal Haig, issued the desperate order:

"With our backs to the wall and believing the justice of our cause, each one of us must fight to the end."

Allied command feared the loss of the channel ports, from which troops and supplies were brought over to the Western Front from Britain. The danger to the French was much more severe. By the beginning of June, the German army had reached the river Marne and they were within 40 miles of Paris. The roads became congested with French civilians escaping from the fighting.

The French troops were depleted and discouraged, unable to find the will to fight the gigantic German army arranged before them. With these desperate circumstances, the British and French generals turned to the American Expeditionary Force. They were the first wave of American troops that arrived in Europe to save the day.

The command of the AEF was under John J. Pershing. He understood the British and French Allies had all but lost the will to wage war. This meant the burden of winning the war was now on his shoulders with his fresh and enthusiastic troops. He found commanding his army in Europe to be frustrating. We were not welcomed as equal partners. The Allied generals talked down to Pershing and his staff. They guessed the Americans were inexperienced and naive, which of course, we were to an extent.

In particular, the Europeans believed the American soldiers didn't have the will or motivation to fight. I remember hearing a story of the Commander in Chief General Pershing banging his fists on the table in a rage and shouting:

"I'm certainly going to jump down the throat of the next person who asks me, 'Will the Americans really fight?'"

The fault for this lack of understanding and trust between the three sides didn't entirely lie with the Europeans. Throughout the war, the British and French fought together as allies. The Americans on President Wilson's insistence didn't wish to be considered allies. They preferred the term co-belligerents. We came to fight alongside the Allied French and British, not underneath them.

During the Ludendorff offensive, drastic combined action was called for. For the entire duration of the crisis, the Allied forces were placed under the command of one of the veteran French commanders.

It was May 1918, when we first engaged the German army and heavy fighting began. It was at a small village near the river zone. Over a third of American forces were killed or injured in just three days of intense combat. It was more than enough to prove that we were capable of fighting with as much determination as anyone.

At the end of May, General Pershing was asked to send soldiers to plug weak spots in the Allied front lines as the German army approached. French troops fled alongside with a desperate stream of terrified civilians that clogged the roads away from town. The nearest American soldiers, the second and third divisions, were over 100 miles away. We had to make an exhausting overnight journey, and then we were expected to begin fighting as soon as we got there. As we approached our destination, the roads became thicker with fleeing French troops and civilians. They kept shouting at us; you're too late. You're too late. It didn't really help to boost my confidence. When we arrived at the almost deserted town on June 1, we found a small number of

African troops defending it. They were left behind by their French colonial masters to fight and die in an impossible situation.

Now they were joined by our 17,000 troops from both the Army and the Marines. The battle for the town was intense, but we held on, and the fighting spilled into the nearby small towns close to the Belleau Wood. It was a dense, almost impregnable area of forest and rock that was around a mile long. Belleau Wood had no strategic value. The German troops were dug in and had set up defensive positions there in early June. It was going to be an effective base from which to harass us. Allied commanders decided that the Germans must be destroyed and driven out, especially because of their machine-gun fire from cleverly hidden positions in the thick undergrowth.

The whole time we'd been in the Belleau Wood, it hadn't stopped raining. Artillery fire fell on us constantly. German planes swooped down from the sky and strafed us, it was difficult to shake off the feeling that we were facing a superior enemy in strength and experience.

We were out to prove ourselves.

We were fighting fresh, well-armed and determined to win. When a French senior officer suggested to a Colonel of the fifth Marines that we should withdraw, he spat, and said:

"Retreat? We just got here."

We had a particularly difficult journey to the battlefront and for many of us, it was our first time in combat. We'd been dropped about 20 miles from the fighting and had to march for over two hours uphill. All around us, French artillery fired a constant barrage over the German lines and the ground constantly shook.

Our men were exhausted, drenched and hadn't been able to wash or shave for at least five days. We finally arrived at the rendezvous point and were transferred to trucks, which carried us to the front. Once there were sent to a small town right next to the Belleau Wood. Above the woods, we spotted German observation balloons, which we nicknamed sausages because of their shape.

This wasn't good news.

Certainly, we'd been spotted, and they were waiting for us. The Germans began to shell us hard and practically destroyed the town. There was a building on my right burning, and the flames lit up the ground around me. All I saw was dead Marines lying in this narrow road.

Then they ordered my battalion into the Belleau Wood. At three o'clock we started for the front trenches. We were supposed to reach the front lines before daylight. The Woods were so dense; it seemed almost impossible to make our way through. The limbs of the trees kept hitting us in the face. Men were cursing. After a depressing night of trekking, we reached the frontline trenches. The Germans continued to shell us, a shell hit close caving in our dugout and killed a friend of mine by the name of Burke.

The piece of shrapnel just took his whole head off.

The trenches I found myself in were barely waist-high. After a thoroughly exhausting day, we had to try to sleep while crouching in ankle-deep water. Over the next few days, the Germans launched night attacks on us. Once, when a soldier threw a grenade at approaching Germans, it bounced off a tree and landed back in his trench. I saw it just in time to hit the bottom of my trench to keep from getting killed. I laughed like a fool while the soldier on the other side of me cursed like a sailor, he came close to getting killed by one of our own men.

On June 6, we were involved in a particularly costly assault on the woods. We were ordered to charge against well-defended German positions over an open field. We were pinned down by heavy fire during this attack. A marine veteran, Sergeant Dan Daly, coined his forever winning phrase:

"Come on ya sons of bitches, do ya want to live forever?"

Luckily, there was a journalist on hand to capture the moment. Daly's immortality and Marine Corps folk law was assured from that moment. It was that type of gung-ho bravery in the face of daunting odds that the Marines were supposed to be all about. Sergeant Daly survived the attack and the war, although he was wounded in the fighting at Belleau Wood.

What followed this battle was the worst single day of fighting in Marine Corps history. There were over 1,080 men killed or wounded. Fighting for possession took on a claustrophobic grizzly quality. Inside the combined battleground, dense underbrush obscured the ground between the trees with huge boulders complete with their own little nooks and crannies. The entire battle was fought in an atmosphere of chaos. So dense were those woods.

Enemies passed within inches of each other. We couldn't see our fellow soldiers and had to be careful to not to shoot our own men. Both Germans and Americans poured into this confined place. The ground between the trees were thick with fallen bodies. You could see the personal debris of these dead soldiers, knapsacks, letters from home, tattered uniforms, they all blew around in the wind. It was the pathetic remnants of their young lives and dark omens for those who were still alive. Hand grenades, machine guns, explosive shells, gas, all stripped the leaves from the trees.

When we met the enemy, it was often in that most dreaded form of fighting hand to hand combat. We fought with brass knuckles bayonets in a hideous device, we call it a toad sticker. It was a long triangular blade attached to a knuckle handle. A friend of mine, a marine private, who'd been in the thick of the hand to hand fighting for over 15 minutes before surviving all his German opponents. He wrote in a letter home about the awful psychological strain that that combat caused with him. After the fighting was over, he sat down and just cried. Having to hold on to such a tightly confined space was an unnerving experience.

Shells steadily fell on our positions. Machine gun and rifle fire continually sprayed through the trees, bringing down chunks of rock, earth, and splintered wood on us. The Germans fired trench mortars at us to black projectiles over four feet long packed with high explosives. We call them aerial torpedoes. Gas shells also landed in the woods, leading pockets of highly Noxious Fumes that lurk low in the ground. The gas would often be harmless, but it would catch sleeping, resting Marines lying in shallow foxholes, and leave them choking and retching.

There was one occasion in the middle of a gas attack when a Gunnery Sergeant gave his gas mask to a wounded marine. That Gunnery Sergeant died a painful death a few days later, his lungs destroyed by the gas. The shell blasts hammered our eardrums in the woods until my ears sang in a constant, disorientating hum. But often, the shell fire was ineffective. The concentration of trees and vegetation muffled the blast of the shells. The visibility was poor, and we were on the edge of the woods.

We followed the course of the battle by listening to the

ghastly procession of noises. From time to time, there'd be a rapid ripple of machine gunfire. This could only mean that Marines were attacking a machine gun nest. They were surely dying as they rushed it, followed by an ominous pause. Then, the machine gunners would be killed by bayonets and trench knives, the silent weapons of hand to hand fighting.

By June 11, we'd captured two-thirds of the woods, but we were now close to physical exhaustion. The Germans counter-attacked and the intense fighting continued. Corpses piled up inside the woods, and Marines picked their way past the bodies of the enemy.

Occasionally, a German soldier would hide in the heaps of dead and rise behind to shoot one of our men in the back. Belleau Wood was packed with snipers, hidden in the high trees and undergrowth. These brave men handpicked for a job that promised almost certain death, or an ever-present hazard. When the machine-gunning and shelling died down in the woods, it took on a sinister silence. As if this wasn't enough, it was easy to get lost in such thick woods. There were few landmarks in a man could lose all sense of direction. Soldiers had to carry a compass to make sure they returned to their own lines rather than the enemy.

On June 23, we withdrew our troops and bombarded the forest for a full 14 hours. Then we entered again in force and fought for another two full days to try to rid the Belleau Wood of German troops. Fighting was so heavy that over 200 ambulances were needed to carry away the wounded. Eventually, on June 26, Belleau Wood finally fell into our hands.

It had taken an agonizing 25 days, but and Belleau Wood was one of the most significant battles of the war. If we hadn't halted the German advance, they could have carried on to Paris.

But for our victory, we paid a terrible price.

A third of all men who took part in this battle were killed or wounded. One company lost 235 of its 240 men. Belleau Wood showed that the American military meant serious business. We would fight a hard war and casualties would be high. By the time the war ended, over 150,000 American soldiers and marines had died, and over a quarter million were wounded. Our Marines were immensely proud of their victory at Belleau Wood.

Now, over a century later, the battle is still a cause of resentment. Some historians feel marines should never have been sent into the woods. Similar fighting between British and German soldiers in heavily wooded areas resulted in high casualties.

Today, the forest looks beautiful and is a popular spot for family picnics. The sun shines through the branches, giving a luminous glow to the green moss growing on the trees. And still, a hint of fleeting warmth lingers over the dark brown carpet of leaves that cover the ground.

WAR TO END ALL WARS

B arely a year after the conflict ended, a journalist for the London Times coined the term:

"The First World War."

Like many others, he'd realized that the war that would end war would actually become the major cause of another world war in the future.

Even when the warring nations were conducting peace negotiations in Paris 1919, their leaders knew that the peace they were making wasn't going to last. The French Supreme Commander dismissed the proceedings as a twenty-year ceasefire. The British Prime Minister Lloyd George said:

"We'll still have to do this whole thing again in twenty-five years and at three times the cost."

He was right. The second world war broke out nearly twenty years later and claimed four times as many lives. So, the most terrible war in human history had a fitting conclusion. It bred another that would be even worse.

The decision reached in Paris to make Germany pay was short-sighted. Germany was forced to make payments of billions of dollars known as reparations to the victorious nations. The American delegates never agreed to this idea, but France, in particular, insisted on prompt payment.

As the war ended, Germany was hovering on the brink of a communist revolution. The country suffered the shame of defeat, lost territory and their economy was ruined by war and reparations. The German population was outraged. They had won the war in the east, and the war in the West had ended before Allied soldiers invaded Germany.

How could it possibly be claimed that they had lost the war?

Their bewilderment was especially intense because German newspapers hadn't reported the full extent of the German army collapse. In the 30s, a former frontline soldier by the name of Adolf Hitler capitalized on this source of resentment. His Nazi Party came to power 1933 and set in motion the events that caused the Second World War.

For some, it was duty, patriotism, or the belief that they were fighting for a better world. For others. It was the simple fact that they'd be imprisoned or shot and a disgrace to their families if they did not.

Men who survived the war expected some reward for their efforts. Most were disappointed. The world left Russia with a Bolshevik government, which inflicted famine, murderous purges and severe oppression on its population for over 70 years.

France had won, but it was hardly worth the price. It never recovered its position in the world as a great power.

The war left Britain and the British Empire with over 940,000 dead and an economy close to break down.

Only America had done well, emerging as the world's strongest and richest nation. In another twist of fate, just as the conflict ended a colossal influenza epidemic swept through the world. Weakened by the stress and deprivation of four years of war, over 10 million people died.

Those who survived the war suffered its consequences for the rest of their lives. Soldiers with lungs ruined by gas or missing three or even four limbs slowly faded away into nursing homes. All through Europe, asylums were full of men suffering from shell shock. Today this is a psychological condition and recognized in combat soldiers as PTSD. But in 1918, military tradition and society were only a couple of years from believing that such men should be shot for cowardice.

There's still men and women alive today whose fathers were shot during the war because they suffered mental breakdowns brought on by the strain of fighting in the trenches. Even those who suffered no apparent physical or psychological damage were tormented by what they had seen and done. One in eight men who fought in the war were killed. Most were under 30, and many still in their teens.

Hundreds of thousands of women around the same age were unable to marry because there simply weren't enough men to go around. The war is now part of our history and it is still part of living memory. In 1998, at the 18th anniversary of the armistice, there were 160 men still alive in Britain who had fought in the Great War. Perhaps similar numbers existed in Germany, France, America and Russia.

By now, in 2020, I'm sure all of them will have died. World War One is still a frequent topic of novels, films and television documentaries. It's difficult to find anything positive to say about it. But perhaps those of that luckless generation born at the end of the 19th century would take comfort from the fact that the slaughter they endured still haunts us today.

A stark reminder of the horror of war.

WWII

More than 75 years now divides us from World War II. Movies, documentaries, and books still produced on the war show it continues to wield a compelling interest.

Today, those who fought in the war are disappearing. Many people still have grandparents or other family who remember it as children. The conflict is not some distant history. It's still within graspable living memory. These stories will touch on different aspects of the war. There are some epic naval battles between titanic warships and monumental battles between armies of hundreds of thousands of men. There's also single-handed duels between snipers and other tales of brave men facing almost certain death in a war-torn world.

For those who survived the war, it was the most extreme and dramatic experience of their lives. Most of the young men who perished were in their early 20s or even late teens. WW II was fought between two great powers. On one side was the Axis Powers: an alliance of Germany and Japan, Italy, also joined by Hungary, Bulgaria and Romania. On the other hand, were the allies Britain and her Empire, Russia and the United States.

These enormous forces faced off against each other in five primary areas of fighting: North Africa, the Soviet Union, Eastern, and Western Europe, and Southeast Asia. The cause of the war is too complex to reduce to a simple explanation. But in essence, the Second World War was caused by the desire of the Axis Powers, principally Germany, to gain empires and the unwillingness of the allies to allow it to happen.

Nazi dictator Adolf Hitler dreamed of living space in Eastern Europe and Russia for his Aryan German race. Mussolini dreamed of creating a new Roman Empire for Italy. Japan sought to take over the Asian and Pacific territories from the fading European powers that seized their empires in past centuries.

The war officially began with the German invasion of Poland on September 1st, 1939. Proud Polish cavalry charged against German tanks with predictably disastrous results. The War ended on September 2nd, 1945, six years, and a day later.

Japan eventually surrendered following the destruction of two of her cities by atomic bombs. At the beginning of the war, Germany and her allies made spectacular advances, and nearly all of Europe fell under her control. This was due to the effective fighting tactics used by the German army and their lightning war, *Blitzkrieg.*

Tanks, newly designed aircraft and other powered vehicles crushed and obliterated opposing armies. In the first two years of the war, only Britain held out. They were protected from invasion by their Air Force, Navy, and the English Channel. The battle for Britain, the first significant aerial battle in history, was also Hitler's first defeat.

With Britain isolated, helpless and confined to her island, Hitler turned to his chief ambition, the conquest of Soviet Russia. The invasion on June 22nd, 1941, was history's grandest. By autumn of that year, German troops were already at the gates of Moscow and Leningrad. Only due to a suicidal resistance by the Red Army, and the onset of the ferocious Russian winter stopped Hitler from snatching his prize on the other side of the world.

Germany's ally, Japan, had established her Empire in the Asian Pacific. On December 7th, she attacked the sleeping giant, the United States at Pearl Harbor. This began a devastating campaign, which saw Japan's army sweep through the Philippines, then down to Burma and Java, to threaten both Australia and India. After Japan attacked the US, Hitler also declared war on the Americans, even though he still had to defeat the British and the Russians.

Winston Churchill was ecstatic. He said:

"So we had won the war after all, our history will not come to an end, and Hitler's fate is sealed. As for the Japanese, they'll be ground to a powder. All the rest was merely the proper application of overwhelming force."

Winston Churchill was right. Japan and Germany had decided to wage war against the most powerful nation on Earth. The United States responded to their challenge by diverting her vast industrial strength to winning the war. In over three years, her dockyards built over 1,200 new warships. By mid-1944, the United States produced one new warplane every five minutes. And aside from the significant expenditure, over $2 billion was still found to fund the development of the world's first atomic weapons.

By the summer of 1942, the United States, British and

Commonwealth troops began to claw back territory seized by Japan in the first six months of the war. In North Africa, a British victory against German and Italian soldiers in October 1942, removed any possible idea that the Japanese and German troops could link up in India. This victory also allowed for the British and American invasion of Italy from the south, which took place in July 1943.

During 1942, the Soviets began to recover from their invasion in the previous year. Now, their armies were better equipped, both from their factories and the substantial American and British arms imports. The Soviet soldiers had now become a formidable fighting force. When Russian troops destroyed the German Sixth Army at Stalingrad over the winter of 42 to 43, the war in the East turned into a slow retreat that ended with the Soviet occupation of the German capital, Berlin.

On June 6, 1944, British, Canadian and American troops took part in the D-day landings in Normandy. Now, Hitler's armies had to fight on three fronts. They were engaged in Eastern Europe, Western Europe, and Italy. Within a year, the war in Europe was over, and Hitler committed suicide on April 30th, 1945. On May 8th, Germany surrendered.

Japan held out until the summer when devastating atomic bomb attacks on Hiroshima Nagasaki and forced them into surrender. Famous novelist John Steinback summed up the war:

"As dirty a business as the world has ever seen..."

That seems a fair accounting, at least 55 million died as a direct result of World War II.

SINK THE BISMARCK

It was early May 1941. Our crew on the *Bismarck* feverishly prepared for inspection by none other than our führer, Adolf Hitler. Now, here among us. Our decks scrubbed and rails polished, our uniforms pressed, and the ship's barber had worked his way through as many of the 2,000 men as time and his blistered fingers allowed.

This was a visit by the führer to Germany's greatest battleship. Our crew, with an average age of 20, was immensely proud of their new vessel. I watched as the führer passed through the assembled ranks. We stood, faces stiff with pride, and awed to be in the presence of our leader. Hitler was not impressed with everyone on parade. He walked by a fellow anti-aircraft gunner, and the führer looked straight through him. I'll never forget the shark-like, cold, and heartless eyes that I saw that day.

The führer had an almost schoolboy fascination with our battleship and went on a tour. He was mesmerized with the *Bismarck's* gunnery control system. Its state-of-the-art computer mechanism took in the ship's speed and course and that of its enemy, wind direction as well as shell flight time. This produced changes of correction of aim at what was by the standards of the time—lightning speed.

Hitler also noted with pride, the two huge swastikas, the emblem of his Nazi Party, painted at either end of the ship, which served to identify the vessel to their aircraft. We had a small Navy, but our warships were the most advanced in the world, and the *Bismarck* was the pride of our fleet. She was a genuinely colossal war machine, over a sixth of a mile long, and bristling with massive guns. She was no doubt the fastest, best armed, and most protected battleship of her day.

The *Bismarck's* most senior officers accompanied Hitler on his tour of inspection. The captain was a stiff, frail-looking 45-year-old man who was never without a cigarette. In his portrait on the ship, he stared out at the world with piercing intelligent eyes. His blond hair slicked back behind two enormous ears. But his slightly comical and stern look was misleading. We held him in high regard and affection. We even referred to him behind his back as *our father*. He emanated both confidence and approachability. Being anointed captain of the Bismarck was the most significant break of his naval career.

With him was our Fleet Commander, together with 50 of his staff. Our Fleet Commander, Admiral Lütjens, was a handsome 51-year-old man. He had a stark resemblance to American film actor Lee Marvin. Admiral Lütjens, like many officers in the German navy, was not a great supporter of Hitler and had tried to protect Jewish officers under his command. Right from the start of the war, he believed Germany would be defeated. Maybe that was why he was such a forbidding man to be around, and he seldom smiled or laughed. Although he was an excellent commander, he didn't have the leadership skills as future events will show.

Admiral Lütjens knew that the British feared his powerful ship and that they would do everything in their considerable power to destroy it. More than any man aboard the Bismarck, he did not expect to return from this posting alive. Britain was the only major European power still undefeated by us. Our commander in chief of the Navy, Grand Admiral Raeder, intended to use our Navy to starve their isolated island opponent into defeat. British survival was dependent on cargo ships from the United States. And so far, this tactic was working. It was now early 1941, and two other battleships had ventured out into the North Atlantic on raiding missions and sunk 22 ships between them.

Now, in May of this year, our *Bismarck* was preparing to do the same. The expedition was codenamed *Operation Rhine,* and sailing out with us was another modern ship named *Prinz Eugen*. This raid would be different, on previous raids, our warships were told to avoid battle with the British Navy at all costs. We were to concentrate solely on destroying merchant ships. But now, we were so confident in our new warship that the German High Command had permitted us for us to fight back if we came under attack.

Most of our crew—including myself—felt we were in an invincible battleship. We had no idea of the horrors that awaited us. There were a few more experienced sailors that had been aboard sinking ships and were old enough to know that the British Navy was a formidable foe. Even our Grand Admiral Raeder had admitted his surface vessels in the Navy—as opposed to his lethal submarine fleet—could take part in hit and run raids only.

We were heavily outnumbered by the British, who'd always depended on their powerful fleet to keep control of their sprawling overseas Empire and protect their trade. I remember hearing once Admiral Raeder had heard that we were at war with Britain, he greeted the news with resignation:

"Our surface forces can do no more than show that they can die gallantly."

Almost from the start of our mission, the *Bismarck* and *Prinz Eugen* were shadowed by British planes and ships. They kept carefully out of the range of our guns. When news reached the British Admiralty that our ships had left Norway to venture out into the shipping lanes of the North Atlantic, immediate action was taken. I understood that the Royal Navy ordered two of their most powerful warships, the *Prince of Wales* and the *Hood* to intercept us. These ships slipped away from their Orkney base in the early hours of May 22nd. The *Hood* was quite possibly the most famous battle cruiser in the world. She was built in 1918 and was handsome and a formidably armed vessel. She was also a sixth of a mile from bow to stern.

The *Hood* had become a symbol of British naval power and had a fearsome reputation during our training exercises. Our crew along the *Bismarck* had frequently run through attack and resistance tactics with the *Hood* as our imaginary enemy. Now we were about to fight her for real. We took a course up past the north of Iceland, and through the Denmark Straits, which separate Iceland from Greenland. Here, we sailed by vast sheets of ice that formed around the coastal waters of Greenland for most of the year.

On the journey up, the two deck swastikas were hurriedly covered over with a fresh coat of paint. The only aircraft out here would be British ones. Such an insignia would indicate that the *Bismarck* was an enemy ship. It was in these chilly waters that the *Hood* and the *Prince of Wales* raced to intercept us.

This far north, during spring and summer, night falls for a few hours or not at all. In late May, dawn came before two o'clock in the morning. It cast a pale gray light over a heaving sea, dotted by patches of fog and brief flurries of snow. Our men stationed in lookout posts above the ships longed to scuttle back to their cozy and cramped quarters. A biting wind whipped over the bow and stung our numb faces. This delicate spot near the frozen top of the world was one of the most dismal places on earth.

Aboard the German ships, our crews expected an imminent attack. But we had no idea how close the British were. The cruiser *Suffolk* had sighted us just after 11 a.m. on May 23rd. On our ship, we spent an anxious night. There were several false alarms as sound detection operators picked up the incoming rumble of British engines. But it was only a radio message from German headquarters who had been monitoring British transmissions. They told us that the enemy was almost upon us.

Just after the message arrived, our lookout spotted two smoke trails from the funnels of the approaching British, one on the southeast horizon. And even then, we weren't sure this was an attack. Maybe we were still being shadowed by smaller vessels who were just keeping tabs on us. But by 6 a.m., it was evident that the approaching ships meant to attack us.

We sent a terse radio message to headquarters:

"Engaging two enemy heavy ships."

Then we prepared ourselves for the battle to come. In an often-rehearsed procedure, one ton of high explosive shells was hauled up to the huge gun turrets by a complex system of pulleys and rails from magazines deep inside the hole. On the *Bismarck,* we had monstrous projectiles over 16 inches across and loaded onto guns that were 20 feet long and weighed over 100 tons each. The order was given to fire at 13 miles. At once, all four ships began exchanging broadsides. At these distances, shells would take up to a half a minute to reach their target.

It was just after 6 a.m., the roar of the guns were so loud that they could be heard in Reykjavik, Iceland. After the battle began, it soon became apparent that the *Hood's* reputation had been undeserved. The *Hood* was built just after the First World War. She was given heavy steel protection along her vertical surfaces, back when warship designs assumed enemy shells would travel low and hit their sides. Now, 20 years later, such assumptions no longer applied.

By 1940, warships aimed their shells in high arc trajectories where they'd plunge on top of decks and turrets. These were the *Hood's* weakest spots. The second and third salvo had an astonishing effect on the British ship. We watched in astonishment as our much-feared opponent exploded like a giant fireworks display. The entire front half lifted out of the water and broke the battleship in two. A vast silent sheet of flame shot high in the air. As intense as a blowtorch, and so bright it could be seen over 30 miles away. The Hood turned over and sank in less than five minutes in the bleakest of battlegrounds.

I was later to find out that all but three of the 1,500 men crew died. The *Prince of Wales* veered sharply to avoid hitting the *Hood*. She was in deep trouble herself. Seven shells from the *Prinz Eugen* and the *Bismarck* hit her, including one on the bridge, which killed everyone but the captain. Several of her main gun turrets had also jammed.

The British sensed another catastrophe, and with no chance of destroying either German ship, ordered a speedy retreat.

On the *Bismarck* and the *Prinz Eugen* there was an atmosphere of euphoria. Our crews were led to believe that we were aboard the most powerful warship on the planet, and events proved this to be true, hadn't they? Yet the atmosphere on the *Bismarck's* bridge was strained. The admirals had exchanged sharp words about the wisdom of going after the *Prince of Wales*. Even though she was an easy target, they had decided to stick to their original mission of sinking enemy merchant ships. We weren't prepared to take any unnecessary risks. And there was bad news too. Although the *Prinz Eugen* had escaped unscathed, our *Bismarck* had taken two shells from the *Prince of Wales*. Men were killed, the ship's sickbay was filling up with burned and scalded casualties. The most serious scenario was a shell had sailed clean through the front of the ship close to the bow. It hadn't exploded but left a man-sized hole just above the waterline. Our ship lurched up and down through the choppy ocean, and the sea flooded in and drained out, gradually filling the surrounding compartments with over 2,000 tons of water. Our fuel lines were broken, leaving over 1,000 tons of fuel in the forward tanks cut off from the engine room. The ship was seeping into a sickly brown trail of oil. Part of the ship's engine had also been damaged.

I later found out that news of the *Hood's* destruction caused a sensation across the world. Winston Churchill would recall it is the single worst moment of the war. This was when the British Admiralty issued the famous order: *Sink the Bismarck.*

They sent two battlecruisers, two aircraft carriers, 13 cruisers, and 21 destroyers to avenge the *Hood*. They were sent to find and destroy us, and their first task was to make sure we did not vanish from sight.

The North Atlantic stretched for more than a million nautical square miles. Although we'd still be shadowed by smaller British vessels, it would be easy to lose them. The next morning, the rain and drizzle eventually gave way to an occasional hint of sunshine. But the sea was still heaving. The ship was losing fuel and taking in water. We still had full firepower, but we lacked speed, essential for our hit and run missions. The *Prinz Eugen* was ordered to break away from us and continue alone. We would take our ship to the port of St. Nazaire, France, for repairs. At our current speed, we would make the 1,700-mile journey in just under four days.

Meanwhile, the British relaunched their *Swordfish* Torpedo Bombers from the aircraft carrier *Victorious*. These rickety biplanes looked like relics from the First World War. They slowly lumbered through the sky. We quickly fought off the *Swordfish* with our anti-aircraft guns and put up a protective sheet of flame that prevented the planes from launching their torpedoes accurately. There was one hit, but it caused minimal damage.

Another British aircraft carrier hurried to intercept us, the *Ark Royal*. She would soon prove to be far more deadly. Our Admiral made a midday speech to us over the ship's PA system. The *Hood* was the pride of England; he told us:

> *"The enemy will now attempt to concentrate their forces and set them onto us. The German nation is with you. We will fight till our gun barrels glow red, and the last shell has left the breach. For us soldiers now it is victory or death."*

He wasn't diplomatic with his choice of words, but even admirals are human. And I'm sure he knew what was coming, but in my opinion, he was too pessimistic.

That night we had outrun our British pursuers, and when dawn came, they had lost sight of us. Our Admiralty did not know. Later in the day, our Admiral sent a long despondent message to German High Command. It was picked up by British radio trackers, who concentrated an aerial search in the area where they detected the signal. But even then, luck was still with us. The British fleet miscalculated our position and assumed that *Bismarck* was heading back to Norway rather than France. They altered their pursuit course accordingly.

It would now be a whole 31 hours before the British found us. It wasn't until 10:30 a.m. on May 26th that observing members of the RAF *Catalina* circling just outside of the range of our guns spotted us. The port of St. Nazaire was only a day or so away, as was the imminent prospect of both air and U-boat support. Our position was reported by the *Catalina* and the British fleet altered their course to the south.

The aircraft carrier *Ark Royal* was closing fast. Its huge bulk heaved in the rough sea and torrents of seawater sprayed the flight deck. Ground crews prepared the bulky *Swordfish* bombers by loading heavy torpedoes to the undersides. In the middle of the afternoon, 15 *Swordfish* lumbered into the air. They didn't expect to sink the Bismarck as they hoped, but at the very least, they wanted to cause enough damage to slow us down so that the other pursuing British ships could catch up and attack.

These planes slipped through the low cloud fog, driving rain and pounced, flying just above the waves to unleash their torpedoes against us. If the Swordfish crews were surprised by the complete lack of defensive fire from the ship below, it didn't cause them to pause and consider their target. All their torpedoes missed, which was fortunate for the British because the ship they'd attacked was the British cruiser *Sheffield*.

Despite the humiliation and embarrassment, a second wave of 15 *Swordfish* were sent off into the slow falling dusk. This time they found us. We were only 620 miles from the French port. They moved so slowly. It seemed like they were hanging in the air, but they flew in so low their wheels brushed over the waves. Our guns could only fire above them. This time two torpedoes hit home, one caused only minor damage while the other exploded underneath the stern.

A huge watery explosion shot up like whiplash through the length of the ship. It buckled deck plates and bulkheads and threw men to the floor and against middle partitions with breathtaking violence. Above this side of the explosion, water surged into the ship with a vengeance, flooding the entire steering compartment.

The sea burst through once waterproof compartments and gushed down cable pipes that ran the length of the ship. I heard later aboard the *Ark Royal*, that senior commanders listened to wild, excited reports of their young pilots. They tried to sift fact from fiction to determine what damage had been done. One Pilot's account seemed to indicate something extremely significant. After the attack, the *Bismarck* was seen making two huge circles and then slowed down to a halt. It was obvious our steering had been badly damaged. In fact, the rudder had jammed at 15 degrees to port.

It was now time to put desperate measures into effect. The *Bismarck* carried three seaplanes. Plans were made to remove the hangar door and weld it to the side of the stern to counteract the effect of the rudder. But bad weather made this impossible.

Admiral Lütjens sent another grim signal home. *Ship no longer steering.* German naval authorities reacted by ordering more U-boats to head for the *Bismarck's* position as soon as possible. But our U-boats weren't the swiftest of vessels, and there were none nearby. Another message was sent that the admiral shared with us over the ship's PA. It was from Adolf Hitler, he said:

> *"All Germany is with you, what can be done, will be done. The performance of your duty will strengthen our people and their struggle for their existence."*

This message offered no hope for survival. That night on board the Bismarck was a long dreadful night. I wondered whether I would live to see another dusk. Several men had nightmares, and there were men on other bunks that woke screaming and sobbing. When word spread the rudder was put out of action, the older members of the crew took this to be a death sentence. It was equally strange that later that night, permission was given for the crew to help themselves to anything they wanted, food or drink. It was a blatant admission that the ship was doomed.

We were assured that U-boats and aircraft were heading out to protect us, and some of the younger sailors still hoped that they'd survive after all. That night, the admiral ordered the engines to stop, against the recommendation of the chief engineer. After five nights with virtually no sleep and all the stress and worry of commanding a ship in a now impossible situation, he was a man at the end of his rope.

To keep the crew from worrying too much about the battle to come, the admiral played records of popular songs over the ship's PA system. But his psychological tactics failed. The songs reminded the men too much of girlfriends or wives and families back home.

Admiral Lütjens came up with an idea of getting men with no immediate job to construct a dummy funnel of wood and canvas. The idea was to change the Bismarck's silhouette, so the enemy ships or aircraft would think it was another battleship and leave us alone. This was a considerable task, and men kept busy painting the canvas and building the scaffolding structure all through the night and into the next day.

On the morning of May 27th, we hoped to reach the safety of a French port. But the British fleet closed in to finish the job. Aboard our ship, our exhausted lookouts saw two massive ships heading straight for us. We identified them as *King George V* and *Rodney*, boldly closing in to scare our crew, and it worked. The battle that followed, which started with a salvo from *Rodney* at 8:50 a.m., was brutally effective. As they homed in, the British ships took carefully timed evasive action, darting one way, then another to avoid our powerful guns.

This time, luck was with the British, and few of our shells found their mark. By 9 a.m., *King George V* and *Rodney* were both firing steadily at us. It was nearly four salvos a minute that fell around our ship, which was now entirely obscured by a smoking spray. A huge towering column of water was sent into the air by near misses. A shell hit our ship near the bow. A blinding sheet of flame momentarily swallowed the entire front end of the Bismarck. This one shot, ten or so minutes into the battle, was the most crucial of the day. After that, our two front turrets fired no more. In that one explosion, perhaps half the ship's crew had been killed.

Only one man from the entire front section survived the battle.

Our ship may have been the most technologically advanced battleship in the world, but now we were completely outgunned. For the next hour, hundreds of shells fell on top of us. On deck and below, men were blown to pieces or burned to death. Our interior turned into a blazing deathtrap as the British ships drew closer. Our ship's exceptionally effective construction only made our destruction even more prolonged. As the shelling continued, fierce fires blazed all over our deck and superstructure, and the *Bismarck* began listing to port. It was now 10 a.m., and the British ships were close enough to see streams of men leaping into the sea, trying to save themselves from the flames and still exploding shells. When it was evident that our crew was abandoning ship, the British ordered the shelling to stop.

The *Bismarck* slowly capsized through the carnage, and men ran around blindly, desperately seeking ways to save themselves. Not a single lifeboat, life raft, or even a float remained. All through the smoke and ruin, I saw doctors busy attending to the wounded, giving them pain-killing morphine jabs to ease their agony. Many men were still trapped inside the ship, fires cut off escape routes and shells buckled hatches, which no longer opened. Some were able to escape it by climbing up shell hoists, wiring shafts, or any kind of duct large enough to take them in. Others gave up hope and sat where they could, waiting for the ship to go down, but still, the *Bismarck* stayed afloat.

Finally, at nearly 11 a.m., the *Bismarck* turned over and sank. To this day, it's unclear whether she sank because of the torpedoes or because their crew deliberately flooded her to keep the ship from falling into British hands. I was in the water near the bow and witnessed this one final extraordinary scene. Our Admiral had been killed by shell-fire early in the battle, but the captain had survived. He was with a junior officer standing near the front of the ship with seawater fast approaching. From his gestures, he appeared to be urging this man to save himself, but the man refused and stayed next to the captain. As the deck slowly turned over into the sea, the captain stopped and raised his hand to his cap, gave one final salute and disappeared. I only thought these happened in books and movies, but I saw it with my own eyes.

There were hundreds of us in the water. We had been told that the British regularly shot their prisoners. In retrospect, it was a sly piece of propaganda designed to ensure our military forces would be reluctant to surrender. But we were freezing in the water, and we swam towards the British ships. The British hurriedly bundled us aboard, but in a cruel twist of fate, a lookout spotted a whiff of smoke a couple miles away, which they thought to be a German U-boat.

The British ships were immediately ordered to move off. Although I was one of the hundred men that were rescued, they left 300 more in the water. As I was later to find out, these exhausted men who had seen their hopes of survival raised and crushed slowly succumbed to the intense cold of the ocean. Only five men lived to tell the tale. Three were picked up by a U-boat and two by a German weather ship.

When other German ships arrived on the scene, they found only rubble, lifebelts, and a few floating bodies. I watched the *Bismarck* turn upside down and descend to the ocean floor, three miles below. Her four huge gun turrets fell from their housings. By the time she hit the slopes of a vast underwater volcano, some 20 minutes later, she'd righted herself and set off a massive landslide, which carried her further down the slope.

There she lies to this day, where she was discovered by a marine archaeologist in 1989. His underwater cameras showed the hull remains intact. Shells, barnacles, and other small sea creatures now line the wooden planks of her deck.

DUTCH SPY INCIDENT

It was October 1939, and the Second World War had just begun. I was in a town in neutral Holland. I sat waiting. Suddenly another car drove up and the passenger side door opened. The driver looked like a typical English gentleman. He was tall and had an aristocratic manner. He wore a tweed suit. His hair was carefully oiled, and he wore a monocle.

He was a spy. He lived in Holland with his Dutch wife and ran a small business importing bicycles. He was a member of the Z branch. It was an independent group of agents which formed Britain's Special Intelligence Service, SIS. His credentials were impressive. He spoke four languages and during the First World War, he'd run a successful network of spies behind enemy lines. Now, he was trying to make contact with dissatisfied Germans willing to fight against Hitler and the Nazis. As far as he could tell, things were going very well for him. His name was Evans and he'd been contacted weeks earlier by a refugee who had fled from persecution in Germany.

The refugee said he knew many high-ranking officers within the German army. He'd assured Evans that there'd be a great deal of resentment against Hitler. The bitterness had built up to a strong resistance movement. Evans probed deeper and he was given my name and that I was an officer involved with the resistance movement.

Evans was the man I now sat in the car with. He spoke German well, and we drove through the Dutch countryside chatting about classical music and our dissatisfaction with Hitler. We stopped in a small Dutch town and picked up two more of Evans's colleagues. One was an English officer named Major Stevens, and the other a Dutch officer named Captain Janssen. Although Holland was neutral at the time, Captain Janssen was assisting the British. He wanted to keep his nationality a secret, so he pretended to be Canadian and use the name, Coppin. This was a convincing alias because Captain Coppin lived in Canada for several years, and the country was an ally of Britain.

As Evans drove on, I reeled off a list of officers who were eager to see Hitler's downfall and named a distinguished general who was prepared to lead the resistance. I promised to bring the general to the next meeting, which we set for October 30. What Evans didn't know was that we were one step ahead of him. The refugee who'd introduced him to me was, in fact, a German spy. The resistance movement I was telling Evans about didn't exist. I didn't exist as he knew me either. I was really Walter Schmidt, A 31-year-old ex-lawyer, now head of German Foreign Intelligence. Instead of being a spy for Evans and the British, I wanted to annihilate them.

My plan was simple. Over the upcoming weeks, I intended to lure the British and the Dutch agents into a false sense of security by pretending to be a willing collaborator. Then I'd bait them into meetings, which would enable me to penetrate the SIS and find out about their operations.

My first task was to convince Evans and the British that I

was genuinely working against the Nazis. When I returned to Holland from Germany on October 30, I brought two army friends. One of the men was silver-haired with old-fashioned elegance. This gave the illusion that he might be a disgruntled aristocrat seeking to overthrow the Nazis. It was a plausible disguise because many upper-class Germans did regard Hitler as an upstart.

We crossed the border and drove to a small Dutch town where Evans had agreed to meet us. But as we arrived, he wasn't there. We waited for over an hour. Right before we were about to leave, we saw two figures approaching our car. These were not the British agents we were expecting. They were Dutch police officers, and they got into our car and ordered us to drive to the police station. This isn't what I planned at all. We were meant to be deceiving them and now it looked like they'd caught us.

I was the head of the German foreign intelligence and quite a prize. At the Dutch police station, we were searched. Our clothes and luggage were gone over from top to bottom. This was nearly our undoing; in one of my accomplice's bags laid on the table open and ready for inspection was a small packet of aspirins. Unfortunately for us, these weren't any old aspirins. These were type issued to the SS and bore the official SS medical office label on them. When I spotted the pills, I turned white with alarm and felt my face flush and heart race.

I looked around the room and noticed that the police officers searching the luggage were occupied with another bag. I swiftly snatched the aspirins and swallowed them wrapper and all. The bitter taste was still in my mouth. There was a knock at the door, and it was Captain Coppin and Evans. My stomach dropped, and I felt beads of sweat pouring down my face. Luckily for us, Captain Coppin had come to our rescue. He apologized for the trouble and explained it was all an unfortunate misunderstanding. But I'm no fool. He knew exactly what was going on. The British and the Dutch still suspected us and this whole exercise had been a test to see if they could expose any Germans. If the police had found anything suspicious, such as those SS aspirins, we would have most certainly been arrested.

In a lucky twist of fate, the paper and silver foil of the aspirin wrapper prevented my stomach from absorbing the drug, which would have severely damaged my body. After that, everything went smoothly. We were driven to the SIS headquarters in the Hague and wined and dined like we were visiting royalty. The next day, I was given a radio and a call sign. We were told to keep in contact by radio and that a future meeting would soon be arranged. We shook hands and were driven back to the German border. Over the next few weeks, I was in daily radio contact with Evans' group. Two more meetings were held, and I felt confident they'd accepted me as a genuine spy. But then, a major fly landed in my ointment, and flies didn't come much bigger than Henrich Himmler, the head of the SS.

There was an assassination attempt on Hitler. A bomb exploded shortly after he left the Nazi Party celebration in Munich. Hitler was convinced the SIS was behind the plot and wanted Evans and his men captured immediately. I protested that this would ruin my carefully thought out plan. I said to Himmler:

"The British are completely fooled. Just think of all the information I'll be able to extract."

Himmler was brusque in his reply:

"Now you listen, there's no but—there's only the Führer's order which you will carry out."

I had no options, so I devised a new plan. I had already arranged my next meeting with the British at a small town on the Dutch-German border. I contacted Captain Müller of the SS and arranged for a squad of 12 men to accompany him. We only had time for a quick briefing and then sped off to the border. The captain of the 12 SS men was a thuggish character and had a nickname as the man who started the Second World War.

Two months earlier, Captain Müller handpicked a squad of men dressed as Polish soldiers and staged a fake raid on a German radio station at the German-Polish border. This allowed the Nazis to claim they'd been attacked by the Poles. An excuse to offer the world for invading Poland, which they'd always wanted to turn into a German colony. This German captain was not impressed with me.

I heard he called me behind my back a *pasty-faced, namby-pamby little man.* He wondered how I'd cope with the dangerous business we were about to undertake. The rendezvous with the British was set for 2 p.m. at a small cafe situated in No Man's Land, between the Dutch and German border. I was feeling queasy, and I ordered a brandy to steady my nerves. At almost 3:30 p.m.—an hour and a half late—I saw the British car come into sight. It turned into an alley by the cafe. Evans and Captain Coppin got out. A third man stayed in the car. As I walked over to greet them, I heard the *bang-bang* of shots ring out, and a car roared down the street.

Captain Müller and the twelve SS men who'd been lurking on the other side of the border had driven straight over firing at the British car. This broke all rules of neutrality. Holland was not at war, and German soldiers had no right to cross that border.

It was instant chaos. Captain Coppin drew his pistol and fired at me. I flung myself to the side; an SS car pulled up at the end of the alley. Soldiers hung from the doors with machine guns. Captain Coppin ducked and shifted his aim. He fired, then let loose another shot, narrowly missing the SS Captain Müller in the front seat of the car. He jumped out and returned fire from behind the open door. Men scattered for cover, their guns blazing. The SS Captain ran up and shouted in my face:

"Get out of here. It's a miracle you haven't been hit."

I jumped around the corner to avoid the shots and ran head-on into another SS soldier. This man wasn't at the briefing and didn't recognize me. He assumed I was one of the British. The soldier grabbed me and stuck a pistol in my face. I told him not to be stupid and put the gun away. We struggled and then the soldier pulled the trigger. I grabbed his hand and felt the bullet skim past my head. At that same moment, the SS Captain ran up and told the soldier he had the wrong man.

He probably saved my *namby-pamby life* that day. I peered around the corner and saw Captain Coppin make a break for it. He was hit and limped to get across the street. Spent shells pumped from his pistol as he fired, but it was no use. A burst of machine-gun fire brought him to his knees, and he crumbled into a heap. As he fell, SS men dragged Evans into their car. Soldiers picked up Captain Coppin and tossed him into the car like he was a sack of potatoes. He was already dead. The German cars sped off to the border with a roar of over-revved engines, burned rubber tattooed into the asphalt road.

In the moments after they left, a strange silence hung over the scene. Passersby and border guards emerged from doorways and blockhouses and stood open mouth and motionless. Engine exhaust, burnt rubber, and an acrid tang of spent bullet cartridges hung in the air. Dark red blood-stains littered the road, glistening sickly in the autumn afternoon.

The operation was a huge success. We'd learned much about the methods of the SIS and we had obliterated Z branch in Holland. They were a significant threat to the Nazi Party and had been put out of operation for good, and the war was only two months old. The Dutch spy incident was easily the British Secret Service's most embarrassing blunder of the entire war, and it had huge repercussions. Hitler used the event to justify the German invasion of Holland in 1940. He claimed that it proved the Dutch weren't neutral after all.

When Germans who were genuinely opposed to Hitler tried to contact the British intelligence agents later in the war. They were treated with such a suspicion that nothing ever came of their approaches.

Following his capture, Evans was interrogated at length by the Germans and gave much away. Evans even carried a list of all the British agents in Holland when he fell into the German trap. He was sent to Sachsenhausen concentration camp, where he remained for the rest of the war. He was freed when the camp was liberated by American soldiers in April 1945.

GERMAN SUBMARINE U-110

I peered through the periscope of my submarine *U-110*, it was late morning and foggy on May 9, 1941. Through my narrow lens just above the choppy sea south of Iceland, I saw a convoy of British ships heading toward Nova Scotia.

My wartime service with the German submarine fleet was brief but glorious. In 10 patrols, we'd sunk over 20 ships and damaged at least another four, and we were only a year into the war. I'd been awarded the *Iron Cross*, 1st and 2nd class and the *Knight's Cross*, one of the most prestigious awards for a German military man. I developed a reputation for being insolent with my senior commanders. It was shocking to me why anyone would volunteer to serve on submarines. They were uncomfortable and dangerous.

The reason I did was because German submarines were so devastatingly effective. Throughout the war, our U-boats sank over 2,500 cargo ships and 175 of their warship escorts. But for all the success we had, we paid a terrible price. Two out of three U-boats were sunk, and we lost over 26,000 men to the bottom of the sea.

Our U-boats kept in touch with headquarters through

radio signals. We'd report our progress, positions and receive instructions on where to head next. These reports were always sent in code. It was a code that'd puzzled the British. Their Intelligence Service set up a special code-breaking department to try to crack it. If the British knew where we were in our U-boats, or where we were going, they could avoid us or even hunt us down. Britain depended on food and supplies brought in by ships. Finding a way to crack the German code was a priority for them.

I was ordered to carry out a daytime attack. I felt uneasy. We usually didn't carry out daytime attacks, especially on convoys protected by warship escorts. It was more difficult for escorts to locate our submarine during a night attack. But the fear of losing contact with my quarry overrode any considerations. Just before noon, we unleashed three torpedoes; two of them hit home, sending a tower of spray into the air by the side of two unlucky ships. I ordered a fourth torpedo to be fired, but it failed to leave its launch tube. This at first seemed like a minor mishap, but it ended up turning into a major disaster for our submarine.

When a torpedo is fired, the water is pumped into the forward ballast tanks to compensate for the missing weight and keep the submarine level under the water. Even though the fired torpedo failed to leave its tube, water poured into the front of the vessel and unbalanced the submarine. Our crew fought to regain control. During the ensuing disorder, several other British warships charged towards our U-boat. Only when we had regained control of our submarine was I able to check the periscope.

I saw a warship bearing down on us and I decided to dive deeper under the sea. This was the procedure for a submarine under attack. But it was too late. Inside the hull, the crew listened to the dull throbbing of approaching propeller blades. Then came the splashes of depth charges that were pitched overboard. My mouth went dry and an awful tightness hit me in the pit of my stomach. I waited for the charges to float down toward us.

The explosions roared and the submarine rocked back in forth as if caught in a hurricane. Main lights went out and for a second, there was total darkness. Then our blue emergency lighting flickered on. My eyes adjusted to the dim light, I was terrified, and I felt disoriented. I'd been under attack before and always played my part to perfection. I leaned casually against my periscope mount and pushed my hat to the back of my head. I warned the crew that if anyone on the submarine panicked and started yelling, the British ships would detect our location with their equipment, and home in on us rapidly.

A deathly quiet settled over the submarine. Only the occasional ominous creaking and damage reports disturbed the noise. Neither depth charge had hit our submarine directly, but the damage they caused was still considerable. The trim controls which kept the submarine underwater had broken and the rudder no longer worked. The batteries were now contaminated and covered with seawater, and we gave off a poisonous chlorine gas. The depth gauges gave no reading and we couldn't tell if our submarine was rising or falling to the ocean floor. The worst part was the hissing sound indicating leaks from our compressed air containers. Without this air, the U-110 wouldn't be able to discharge water from the ballast tanks and rise to the surface.

There was no way I could pretend everything was going to be okay. I told my men:

"All we can do is wait now. I want you all to think of home or something beautiful."

These words could not have been much comfort in the awful silence that followed. Maybe my crew thought of how their girlfriends or families would greet the news of their deaths. More likely than not, each man imagined the submarine sinking slowly to the dark depths of the ocean. If a section of the sea was deep, steel plates on the hull would creak and groan. A flutter in the gears told the crew the submarine's air pressure had been disturbed by water pouring into the ship. Then the submarine would wrench apart beneath their feet, and they'd be engulfed by a torrent of black ice water.

At that depth, there was no chance of anyone reaching the surface. If that section of the sea was shallow, the submarine might simply sink to the bottom. Then men would have to sit in a strange blue light or pitch darkness shivering in the damp cold as their submarine gradually filled with water. Then, the corrosive smell of chlorine gas would catch in their throats, and they would suffocate in the foul-smelling air.

Just as these men were convinced they were about to die, *U-110* rocked gently back and forth. A huge wave of relief swept through the men. This was a motion the entire crew recognized; their submarine was bobbing on the surface. I shouted:

"Last stop! Everyone out."

In a well-rehearsed drill, the crew headed for their exit hatches and poured out onto the deck. But our troubles were far from over. As we filled our lungs with fresh air, three British warships bore down on us, intending to ram our submarine before it could do more damage. Shells and bullets whizzed past our ears. None of our men had any intention of manning the guns on the deck or firing any more torpedoes. They just stared death in the face, desperate to abandon the *U-110*. Men jumped overboard and drowned. Others were killed by the shells and bullets that rained down on them. Through the wild confusion, one of our ship's radio operators found me and asked if we should destroy the ship's code books and coding machinery. I shook my head and told him the ship was sinking. Below deck, the last few left aboard opened valves to flood the submarine and make sure it sunk. Then they too jumped into the freezing sea.

* * *

Aboard the HMS Bulldog, we steamed into ram the *U-110* submarine. When I saw that the members of the enemy crew were throwing themselves off the vessel. I ordered our ship to reverse its engines and slowly come to a halt. The other British ships were now certain that the *U-110* was no longer a threat and they stopped firing also.

One of our destroyers pulled up to rescue the German crew. It was our depth charges that had done so much damage. Their submarine captain and fellow officers struggled to stay afloat. I noticed to their horror that the submarine was not going to sink. Clearly, something had stopped water from pouring in. I watched as the submarine commander shouted and tried to climb back on board to sink their boat. But just as he did, a huge rolling wave swept over them, and their U-boat was carried out of reach. The German crew had lost their chance. Most of the men survived long enough in the water to be picked up. The German submarine captain was not one of them.

From our bridge, we surveyed this submarine with great

interest. It was floating low in the water but didn't look like it would sink immediately. Its crew was either killed or being rescued, so it seemed likely to have been abandoned. I was tasked to lead a boarding party of eight volunteers to investigate. We clambered aboard a small boat and were lowered from the HMS *Bulldog,* and set off across the choppy sea. As we approached the black hull of the submarine, my stomach tightened, and I felt tense. I was the most senior officer in the boarding party, and it was my responsibility to lead my men onto the submarine.

The only way in was through a hatch in the conning tower. There could be submariners inside waiting to shoot anyone who entered. It was standard practice on an abandoned submarine to set off explosives on a timer or flood the boat to prevent it from falling into enemy hands. Besides, the crew had utterly abandoned it. It was probably taking in water fast and could sink at any moment. Expecting to die from either a bullet, explosion, or in a torrent of water. I leaped off my boat and onto the slippery deck of the U-110. My men followed immediately behind me, but no sooner had the last men climbed aboard than a wave picked up our boat and smashed it to pieces on the deck of the submarine. This was not a good omen.

With my heart in my mouth, I climbed onto the conning tower to find an open hatch at the top. I stood before it, looking at it, thinking, fighting back my fears, and thinking this was my gateway to doom. I pulled my pistol from its holster and peered down into the darkened interior. There was a gust of warm air that wafted up to meet me. It contrasted against the icy Icelandic wind blowing off the sea and would've been inviting had it not smelled so foul. Submarines have a distinct stench and can be unbearable if you're not used to it. It's the stale, rotten cabbage smell of 40 men confined for weeks on end in an enclosed airless environment, unable to clean their clothes or even bathe properly.

I could sense the impatience of the men behind me. They wouldn't be the first to be shot, but they were just as vulnerable as I was to explosives or a sinking submarine. I swung down into the interior, expecting a bullet right through my rear end. My boots climbed down the long steel ladder, but there was no one there to greet me. I reached the strange blue interior of the control room, and the others followed quickly behind. As their eyes grew used to the dim light, they blundered through the vessel, searching for any remaining crew. But the *U-110* was deserted. My boarding party searched the boat for documents knowing it could still sink or explode at any moment.

Their courage was richly rewarded. Inside the radio operators' cabin was a sealed envelope. It contained codes and other useful information, such as signal logs, instruction procedures, and further codebooks. But there was also a curious machine that looked like a strange sort of typewriter. It had a keyboard, and one of the men pressed a letter on it. A light on a panel above the keyboard flickered on. It was still plugged in. It dawned on me that this was a coding machine, four screws held it to the side of the cabin. These were quickly removed, and the device was carefully put to one side. It was clear there must've been a complete panic among the crew to have left everything behind like this.

As my search party continued, the overpowering dread that we first felt entering the boat had faded. An explosion never came. But there were other things to worry about. The *Bulldog* and other warships guarding our convoy had gone off to chase enemy submarines. If the *U-110* sank in the meantime, we had no boat and no immediate chance of rescue. Finally, the HMS *Bulldog* returned to wait for our boarding party to finish the work. I sat in the U-boat captain's cramped cabin and reflected that my life was starting to look up. When my men had finished their search. They sent a boat to collect us and attached a tow rope to the *U-110*. The next morning the submarine sank in rough seas.

I was upset. A captured submarine was quite a prize and could've been manned by a British crew and used again against the Germans. The news quickly spread that the HMS *Bulldog* had captured a coding machine from the *U-110*. It caused a sensation at British Naval Headquarters and they replied by ordering our crew to maintain the strictest secrecy. When we reached the Navy base at Scapa Flow in Scotland, two naval officers immediately came on board. They were eager to examine the items that we'd seized. The documents also excited great interest. They were thrilled that we had the coding machine, one officer said:

> "We've waited the whole war for one of these."

The next day as the *Bulldog* sailed back to its Icelandic patrol. I received a thinly veiled message from the commander in chief of the Royal Navy. He said:

> "Congratulations, the petals of your flower are of rare beauty."

The typewriter device my party found was a fully working Enigma machine, the ingenious coding instrument devised by the German military. Enigma was used for scrambling a message so that it became diabolically difficult to crack. There were literally billions of possible combinations for each coded message. The Enigma had a keyboard layout like a typewriter, but it only contained the 26 letters of the alphabet. When a letter key was pressed, it sent a signal to a plug bored at the front of the machine. This was arranged in a standard keyboard layout with a variable arrangement of cable leads that could go from any direction. For example, C to V and then from U to K, this was the first stage of scrambling a message.

From the *plugboard,* the signal was routed to a series of replaceable interconnected rotating wheels. Each with all 26 letters of the alphabet around the rim. These scrambled the original letter and were between three and five of these wheels inside the enigma. Depending on the model, the wheels were chosen from a standard selection of eight. From the wheels, the signal was sent to a lamp board position behind the keyboard that lit up another letter, which the operator would then write down. In this way, messages would be fed through for coding and then transmitted via Morse code as regular radio signals.

The Enigma machine was invented in 1919 by a German engineer named Arthur Scherbius. Each keystroke, even of the same key, produced a different letter. If the operator pressed three keys for example, the rotating wheels could create three separate letters, Q, M, and Y. On machines with three wheels, it would not produce the same letter until the key had been pressed over 16,000 times. This was when the internal mechanism returned to its original position.

This type of complexity created its own problems. Messages from one machine to another could only be correctly decoded. If both machines were set up identically, each wheel had to be inserted in one specific position, and in a particular order. This meant the front plugboard had to be arranged in also the same way. This created difficulties for the German Navy. Their ships and submarines would be away at sea for months on end. They were sent out with codebooks that gave precise details on how the Enigma machine should be set up for each day of the week and months ahead.

It would be a disaster for the Germans if such a code-book or coding machine fell into British hands. The machine I captured, and all the accompanying material was sent at once to Bletchley Park. The grand mansion and its grounds were set up as the British intelligence code-breaking headquarters in 1939. Just before the start of the war. The work was done in a makeshift collection of prefab-ricated huts. With collapsible chairs and trestle tables. It was staffed by some of the greatest mathematical minds in the country.

Chiefly run by Alan Turing, a Cambridge and Princeton University professor. His groundbreaking work led to decoding the Enigma messages using primitive computers, which were the forerunners of what we use today. Turing's team had a colossal task. The Enigma code was difficult enough to begin with. But to make it even more difficult, the code was changed every day. And the coding procedures regularly updated throughout the war.

The Enigma machines themselves also went through several design improvements. At the height of the conflict, over 2,000 messages were sent daily from branches of the Armed Forces to Bletchley for decoding. Even with the brightest brains in the country, the staff of Bletchley Park could not crack the Enigma code without direct assistance.

They relied on lucky breaks, and it was myself and my boarding party, which helped them. The books and docu-ments I rescued were especially useful. They gave informa-tion on settings and procedures for encoding the most sensitive top-secret information, which the Germans called officer codes. The Enigma was like a huge jigsaw puzzle. Any codebooks or machines captured help put the puzzle together for a few days or weeks. Until the codes in the machine changed. Instead of decoding sensitive and highly useful messages about U-boat positions or Air Force strikes. Codebreakers would find themselves churning out reams of meaningless gobbledygook.

For the staff at Bletchley Park, these moments were heartbreaking disappointments. They were still well aware of how their work could save the lives of thousands of people. I still wake up at night, all these years later, to find myself going down that ladder. But thanks to the courage of our brave fighting men, the staff of Bletchley Park was provided with further opportunities to break the enemy's code.

THE JEWISH EVACUATION

The snow fell soft and silent around the shores of the lake. It was the morning of January 20, 1942, and a steady stream of chauffeur driven cars arrived at the villa. A succession of the most senior members of the Nazi government and elite SS armed forces arrived and entered the marble entrance hall. Their coats were swept off their shoulders from their aides, and their arrival was silently noted.

There were representatives from the Ministry of Foreign and Eastern territories, the Justice Ministry, the Gestapo the SS, and the Race and Resettlement Office. Most of the representatives had come from nearby Berlin.

Some of the army men were called in from the chaos and horror of the Eastern Front, or from other conquered territory. This tranquil winter scene at the lake must've seemed to belong in some strange parallel universe. The villa where we assembled had marbled staircases and rooms aligned with wooden panels. It was a three-floored mansion that had once belonged to a Jewish businessman. But long since taken over by our government. Looking back, this was to be one of the most sickening conferences in human history.

I oversaw the organization and preparation for the conference. I coordinated the delegates arrival and the staff who attended them. I stood in the doorway as Adolf Eichmann arrived, he was a Nazi in his late 30s, and head of the Gestapo's Jewish affairs section. He was quiet, anonymous, and had the look of a bookkeeper. He didn't radiate the usual charisma and spark of some of his colleagues. He had a reputation for carrying out orders with great efficiency. As the morning progressed, I noted how well our conference was proceeding.

The last to arrive was Eichmann's boss, the SS general Reinhard Heydrich. He was head of the Reich security main office and was one of the most powerful men in the Nazi government. He was tall, blond, handsome, and everything Eichmann was not. He was a former international level fencer and naval officer. He was precisely the *Aryan Superman* from a Nazi propaganda film. In one of his most famous photographs, Heydrich stares out into the distance with a cruel mouth and fierce eyes. He looks to me like a stern headmaster about to administer a severe beating to a gaggle of rebellious students.

There was no doubt that was the image he wanted to project to the world. But in person, Heydrich seemed brisk, efficient, and oozing with charm. Not so for those who crossed him. I heard they found themselves subject to chilling threats made in the casual manner of a Roman Emperor who was secure in his power of life and death over those around him.

As the conference continued, there was a haze of cigarette smoke and the cheerful atmosphere of men who'd had a couple of glasses of wine before lunch. The purpose of the meeting was plain, Heydrich announced that he'd been charged by Hitler's deputy Hermann Göring with the responsibility for finding a solution to the Jewish problem. All the representatives around him were there to ensure the government cooperated effectively with this venture.

All the Nazis at this meeting were distinguished and highly educated men. They were broadly sympathetic to Hitler's corrosive hatred of the Jews. During the several years of Nazi rule, their views were reinforced by a constant barrage of anti-Jewish propaganda. These men had grown to think of all Jews with repugnance and fear. They'd compare the suffering of the Jewish people as one would think of a swarm of diseased rats or even a cancerous virus.

What Heydrich had to report was monstrous. It was so barbaric that he softened his words to the hardline Nazis and used innocent phrases to lessen the impact of what he had to say. He explained to the assembled members with statistics gathered by directly by Eichmann that the German government had a storage problem with the eight million Jews in Nazi territory.

Initially, the Nazi plan was to expel them, but when the war closed the borders, this became impossible. Heydrich led the delegates to the view that the only possible option left to the Nazi government regarding the Jews was *evacuation*. As the conference continued, it dawned on those assembled what *evacuation* meant. They discussed the cold-blooded murder of over eight million people, even 12 million if Germany succeeded in conquering all of Europe.

There were a few objections, even among these types of men. The idea of murder on this scale was too horrific to contemplate. Once Heydrich gained the approval of all the men assembled and his solution was accepted. The delegates in their customary efficiency decided that it would be economically viable to store the Jews in concentration camps. They'd put the men to work on road and factory building projects where natural death from exhaustion and illness would gradually reduce their numbers.

Children, the elderly, and the sick wouldn't be suitable for such projects, and they'd be disposed of as soon as possible. Since the beginning of the war, SS troops in Russia and Poland had been systematically killing Jews by the thousands. Officers reported that their task was unpleasant and demoralizing, especially killing women and children. They decided the most efficient way to murder Jews that couldn't be used for work would be gas. They'd use special camps where hundreds at a time would be herded into gas chambers disguised as shower rooms. Life would be choked out of them efficiently and quickly.

These chambers could dispose of over 700 people an hour, and if they worked around the clock, they'd *evacuate* thousands of Jews a day. The thinking was within a year if everything went to plan. Europe would be *Jew-free*.

After the delegates had all left. Heydrich and Eichmann sat down by the fireplace. They smoked a celebratory cigar and toasted to a job well done. The drink flowed. They sang and danced arm in arm in a jig around the plush chairs and the oak table of the lake house villa.

Four months later, I heard Heydrich was mortally wounded in Prague when he was killed by two Czech soldiers. On June 4, in retaliation, German troops murdered over 1,500 Czechs loosely accused of helping take part in the assassination. They destroyed the Czech village of Lidice, massacred all the males, and sent the women and children to concentration camps.

Immediately following the conference at the lake house, the Jewish evacuation was in full swing. From the Gulf of

Finland to France's Atlantic coast, all the way to the island of Crete, even into the African shores of Libya—all areas controlled by the Nazis—the Jews were rounded up. Some were shot where they stood or gassed in special vans designed for the process. Most were placed on freight trains packed in the hundreds and thousands into cattle wagons and transported to death camps.

Auschwitz, Belzec, Majdanek, and Treblinka. These names would haunt the lives of generations to come and forever be remembered in infamy.

SNIPERS IN STALINGRAD

Even though we failed to conquer Russia, we still had remarkable success. In the summer of 1942, the German army commanded huge parts of Russia. Before the war, 40% of the Russian population lived in the areas the Germans now occupied in the north. We'd reached the city of Leningrad close to the Finnish border and continued down past Moscow to the front.

In the south, we were close to the Volga River and got as far as the Caucasus mountains, only 100 miles from the Caspian Sea. We'd killed millions of Soviet citizens, and millions had fled further east. Now it was August 1942, and after more than a year of fighting, our German Sixth Army was fast approaching Stalingrad. It was named after the Soviet leader Joseph Stalin and the city had great symbolic importance for both the Soviets and us. We were determined to fight as if the outcome of the entire war depended on our victory, and perhaps it did.

I was with the German Sixth Army. As we arrived at the outskirts of Stalingrad, we were foreshadowed by a vast cloud of dust thrown up by our marching feet. The tanks, artillery, and trucks rolled through the parched steppe of late summer. Many of the soldiers were still young, fresh, and in good spirits, the odds were on our side. Most of us who hiked the thousand or so miles from the German border to the banks of the Volga felt we were as invincible as the Nazi propaganda told us.

Our armies shocked the world with our string of victories. But when the Sixth Army got to Stalingrad, we were no longer swept through vast open plains, and we became bogged down in street fighting. It was the kind of warfare that every soldier dreads. Brutal, personal, terrifying hand to hand combat. We fought with bayonets grenades, anything we could grab to kill each other in the most violent, bloody way.

I remember fighting 15 days in a row for a single house. The front was a corridor between burned-out rooms and a thin ceiling between two floors. Our faces were black with sweat. We've bombarded each other with grenades in the middle of explosions. There were clouds of dust and smoke heaps of mortar and floods of blood fragments of furniture and human beings littered everywhere. The street was no longer measured by dimensions, but by corpses.

Stalingrad was no longer a town. It's an enormous cloud of burning blinding smoke, like a vast furnace lit by the reflection of the flames. And when night arrived, the dogs plunged into the river and swam desperately to the other side of the bank. The nights were a terror for them. Animals fled this hell. Only the men could endure.

The battle for Stalingrad raged from August 1942 all the way into February of the next year. It was an exhausting and terrifying battle. The morale of each side would become a deciding factor in the outcome. We arrived convinced that victory would soon be ours. The Russians fought desperately to cling on to what remained of their frontline positions. They must've been in awe of the German Army. We had yet to face serious defeat. There was one point in the battle that over nine-tenths of Stalingrad was in our hands. We were so confident in our victory that the commander of the German Sixth Army had already designed a medal commemorating the capture of the city.

The casualty rate among the Soviet army was incredible. The reinforcements were rushed to Stalingrad to prop up its crumbling barricades. On the other side of the Volga river, they'd be hustled out of cattle wagons and greeted by the scary sight of a city in flames. It looked literally like a vision of hell. From the railhead, men were transferred across the river by ferry. And even if they survived the machine gun and artillery bombardments. The strafing of our *Stuka* dive bombers decimated the new soldiers. They would be lucky to live for 12 hours.

As each area of the city was overtaken by intense fighting, Stalingrad was reduced to little more than a massive pile of rubble. Some of my fellow soldiers described the fight as the *War of the Rats*. Because men scurried and burrowed through the debris. The commander of the Russian forces understood that the key to survival in the city would be through small individual encounters with the enemy, not a war of tanks, artillery, and bombers. He believed the most lethal soldier of all would be the sniper.

In the bizarre landscape of the city with its acres of demolished and burned out factories and apartment buildings, Stalingrad was perfect sniper territory. A soldier could be killed at any moment by a sharpshooter perched atop some derelict building. A handful of good snipers could demoralize an entire frontline regiment. Because of their importance, the Soviet snipers were rewarded well for their efforts. If a Soviet sniper became a marksman with 40 kills, he won the title *Noble Sniper* and was given a medal. Being a sniper is a highly specialized job that requires distinct skills and a unique personality. It's one thing to kill a soldier when he is charging at you with a bayonet. It's an entirely different matter to observe him grimly from a hiding place. You could be talking to a friend, writing a letter, shaving, or even squatting over a latrine. A sniper must kill in cold blood, and at the moment when he's least likely to give away his own position. Sniping is a skill that requires patience and cunning, especially when a sniper is sent to stalk another. Expert knowledge of camouflage is also essential.

At Stalingrad, skilled snipers learned to fire against a white background with a flash of rifle shot that'd be difficult to see. Some snipers improvised special attachments to their rifles—which hid the flash of shot—some setup dummy figures to act as bait regularly returning to move their position.

* * *

It was early September and a desperate time in the battle. It was then that I decided to make a name for myself in the Russian 62nd army. In my first 10 days in the city, I killed over 40 German soldiers. I was a long way from the Elinsky forest and the Ural Mountains. I'd learned to shoot as a young boy and was already a skilled marksman before I joined the army.

Russian propaganda used me for the model of fighting spirit. And because I had the broad open face of a Russian peasant, they put my picture and deeds all over the Russian newspapers. I was now known as the perfect people's hero. But I didn't care about that. I was a sniper. And as my fame grew, my story was also taken up by national newspapers, newsreels, and radio broadcasts.

My success and fame had grown so much that the army set up a sniper training school close to the front, where between forays to the German lines, I'd pass on my skills to eager recruits. Conceal yourself like a stone I told them, observe, study the terrain, compile a chart, and plot distinctive marks on it. You must remember that if in the process of observation, you ever reveal yourself to the enemy. You will receive a bullet through your head for the trouble.

I told my students how to use dummies and other tricks to bait enemy snipers into giving away their position. Sometimes we taught an opponent with a firing range target. Then when we were confident, we'd discovered our enemy's hiding place. We'd hurry back to where the dummy had been and swiftly catch the opponent off guard. This was a common game played between snipers. I warned my students never to become angry at such tactics. The way to stay alive as a sniper was to look before you leap. I told them that a sniper needed to be intimately familiar with the territory in which he operated. Anything different, a pile of bricks here, a slightly shifted pile of wooden planks there, told an experienced soldier that an enemy sniper was lying in wait.

Among my students was a young woman named Tania. She was like many Russian women and fought as a frontline soldier. Most of her family had been killed in the war, and she carried a deep hatred for our German enemy. She called them *targets* and refused to think of them as human beings. She was a talented sniper and often fought alongside me. We shared the hardships of frontline soldiers. We snatched meals with a spoon kept in our boots. We used buckets of cold water to bathe, and we slept huddled together in dark, overcrowded shelters. It was hardly a courtship with flowers and candlelit dinners. But in this brutal, bloody atmosphere of the front with death an instant away. We became lovers.

I was told by Soviet intelligence that the Germans soon learned about me. The German Sixth Army High Command realized what a prize it would be to kill me. Besides the success of our snipers. We were making life so unpleasant for the ground troops that no one dared to raise their head above the rubble during daylight. An SS Colonel named Major Koning was the head of the sniper training school near Berlin. He was flown to Stalingrad, to find and kill me.

He was said to have been the best and had many advantages over the regular Soviet sniper. He knew my techniques because Soviet newspapers and army training leaflets full of my information had been passed on to him. I knew nothing about him. I was just tipped off the Germans had sent their best sniper. For the next few days, I kept my eyes and ears open for any clues as to where this Nazi *Super Sniper* would be. Two of my sniper comrades were shot and killed the next day. They were both excellent snipers, but they were outfoxed by a sniper with even more exceptional talent.

I hurried to the section of the front line where my comrades had been shot. It was in the Red October factory district, a landscape of twisted machinery in the skeletal framework of demolished buildings. I felt like a police inspector investigating a murder. I asked soldiers who witnessed the shootings exactly what had happened, and where my comrades had been hit. I made use of my considerable experience and decided the shots came from a position directly in front of the area where these men had fallen.

Across the lines, through the tangled Rubble, was the hulk of a burned-out tank. This was too obvious a spot for an experienced sniper to lay in wait. But to the right of the tank, there was an abandoned concrete pillbox. The firing slit had been boarded up with a piece of iron, right in front of my own position. This was the perfect spot for sniper hide, and then crawl away and cover of darkness.

I caught sight of the top of a helmet moving along the edge of an enemy trench and reached for my rifle. I realized by the way the helmet was wobbling, it was a trap. Major Koning must've had an assistant who placed the helmet on a stick and waited for me to reveal my position by firing at this dummy target.

I put my theory to the test and placed a glove on the small plank. I raised it above a brick parapet. At once, a shot rang out through the glove and plank in an instant. I looked at the plank carefully. The bullet had gone straight through it. My opponent was obviously directly under an iron sheet. After dark, I scouted the area for a suitable firing spot. That night had occasional bursts of rifle fire, followed by sporadic artillery and mortar barrages every now and then. A flare would shoot high into the air in a graceful arc and float down in a bright blaze that cast harsh shadows over the still sinister landscape.

When the sun rose the next morning, it fell directly on me. I waited to fire. If the sunlight caught my rifle or tele-scopic sight it would have been way too risky. By the early afternoon, the sun moved across to the German lines. At the edge of the iron sheet something glistened in the bright light. Was it Major Koning's rifle, or just a piece of broken glass? I decided to offer the German sniper a target. I care-fully raised my helmet above the broken brick where we sheltered. A shot rang out and pierced the helmet. I rose slightly and screamed as if I had been hit.

Unable to contain his curiosity Major Koning raised his

head a little from behind the iron sheet to get a better look. It was finally the chance I'd been waiting for. I fired one shot, and Major Koning's head fell back. That night I crept up to his position and took his rifle as a souvenir. You can still see the telescopic sight on display at the Armed Forces Museum in Moscow.

The Battle of Stalingrad made up one of the greatest horror stories of modern history. The Germans, along with their Axis Powers, lost over 850,000 men. While we lost nearly three-quarters of a million. Stalingrad was not just the scene of a vast prolonged battle. It was also a city of over half a million people. In the first days of the fighting, nearly 50,000 of them were killed by German bombers, by the end, there were less than 1500 men and women still alive among the rubble.

Some who'd lived in the city before the Germans came, fled east to other parts of Russia. The battle finally ended when our forces outside Stalingrad surrounded the Germans. Not a single healthy man remained at the front in the German Sixth Army. Everyone at least suffered from frostbite. And there were several hundred soldiers who had frozen to death. The German High Command still refused to allow their starving, demoralized Sixth Army to give in. Another two weeks of needless suffering continued before the Germans surrendered. We captured over 90,000 Germans, and less than 5,000 ever returned home. The rest died in captivity.

I looked for Tania shortly after my encounter with Major Koning but heard she'd been critically wounded. She led a small squad of soldiers to assassinate a German Colonel. On the way to the German front lines, one of them stepped on a mine and in the explosion, Tania received a fatal stomach wound.

I was told she was not expected to live. But later I heard she survived. She recovered several months later in a hospital far behind the front lines and also received terrible news. She was told that I was killed in an explosion in the final weeks of the Battle of Stalingrad. I was sunk in despair at the thought of losing her, and for years afterward, I'd just stare into space. Eventually, I recovered and even got married.

This war, like so many others, had consequences I'd bear for the rest of my life.

CODENAME CICERO

I wasn't amused. I was just awoken from a deep sleep and summoned to the house of the first secretary of the German Embassy in Ankara, Turkey—in the middle of the night. What could possibly be this important?

It was early October 1943, and Europe was buried in the Second World War. I was in neutral Turkey. We were uncomfortably positioned between occupied Europe and Soviet Russia, and it was teeming with spies. I was a member of the German Secret Service. My cover was as a trade representative at the German Embassy. I was expected to do odd things at strange times of the day.

I was irritated when I arrived at the house of the first secretary. I found out he'd already gone to bed, and it was his wife who greeted me at the door. She pointed to the drawing-room and told me there's a strange character in there waiting for you. He has something he wants to sell us. Then she returned to bed and reminded me to close the door when I left.

I fumed and briskly walked toward the door to sort out who this visitor was as soon as possible. I searched through the clutter of the room and noticed a still, pale figure sitting on the sofa facing the shadows. I stiffened, and my temper receded. I focused on clearing my head. The man across from me stood up, he was small and squat, had thick black hair and a broad forehead. I remember his face was that of a man used to hiding his feelings. His dark piercing eyes darted around the room, betraying his unease.

He walked over to the door and jerked it open to see if anyone was hiding behind it. My irritation returned. I wasn't one of the Marx Brothers, and this wasn't a comedy film. But from my training, I knew to keep quiet and let the visitor do the talking.

He said:

"I have an offer for you." He spoke in fluent but accented French. *"But first, I must ask you for your assurance that nothing I say will go beyond this room. If you betray me, your life is to be as worthless as mine. I will make sure of that. If it's the last thing I do."*

The man took his pointer finger and drew it across his throat.

I knew I couldn't take a threat like that seriously. But I was a professional spy and my training told me to wait and see what else he had to say before I made any judgments. The man spoke:

"I can deliver you photographs of top-secret information. Extremely top-secret information from the British Embassy. But if you want it, you have to pay me a great deal of money. If I've risked my life for you. I want you to make it worth my while."

I spoke for the first time:

"How much money do you have in mind?"

The man said he wanted £20,000.
I scoffed and said:

"That's completely impossible. What on earth have you got that could be worth such a huge sum of money."

In 1943 that was a fortune. The man puffed his chest out and said:

"Think about it, I'll give you three days to decide, and then I'll call you at the German embassy and identify myself as Pierre. I'll ask you if you have any letters for me. If you say yes, I'll come and see you. If not, you'll never hear from me again. And if you're not interested. I know many others that will be."

Something about this man and his veiled threat made me hesitant to dismiss him. He would undoubtedly take his information to the Soviet embassy in Ankara if the Germans turned him down. I could tell he meant business. I shook his hand and agreed to the arrangement. The man got up to leave, just as he got to the door he turned and smiled with a sly look on his face.

"I bet you really want to know who I am, don't you? Well, I'll tell you. I am the British ambassador's valet."

Before I could say anything else or ask another question, the door slammed shut and this strange little man disappeared. The next morning, I arranged to see the German ambassador Franz von Papen. His demand was so large that we'd have to ask permission directly from the German Foreign Secretary von Ribbentrop himself. I was sure he'd say no. But to my surprise, a reply came back the next morning accepting the arrangement. It said a special courier from Berlin would arrive with the money.

I decided to give this new stranger a codename and called him Cicero after the famous Roman orator. I prepared for his visit. And sure enough, the phone call from Pierre came, and we arranged to meet at the embassy at 10 o'clock at night.

I arranged for a darkroom complete with a photographic technician to be made ready, so I could immediately develop the film. The strange little man turned up five minutes early, and the two of us began a cautious, suspicious exchange. Cicero wanted the money first, and then he would hand over the film. I wanted the film to check if it was genuine. And then I would hand over the money to him. We decided to compromise. I counted out the £20,000 in front of him, and then put it in a safe and took the film to the darkroom.

I developed the film, and the results were spectacular. Unquestionably authentic top-secret documents—all with recent dates. I gave Cicero his money and made further arrangements. We'd pay him £15,000 for every subsequent delivery. This was an astronomical amount of money. But then, this information was extraordinary.

The next time Cicero returned with more film, he asked me to drive him back to the British Embassy. I was astonished. Cicero said:

"But why not. That's where I live."

Throughout the next few months, more film followed. Each revealed highly sensitive documents and information. The German High Command couldn't believe their luck. Cicero was too good to be true. And they started to suspect him playing a game of double agent with them. One where he'd supply false information to confuse and mislead the German Secret Service.

I received orders to find out all I could about our new contact in the British embassy. Cicero's actual name was Eleyza Bazna. He was an Albanian who had made his way to Turkey and settled in Ankara. He found work as a chauffeur and as a valet specializing in high ranking diplomats. He worked for the Slavic ambassador, and another German diplomat who fired him for reading his mail.

Finally, he found work at the British Embassy as a valet for a high-ranking official. Cicero was good at his job. He was efficient, servile, and had a knack for being able to second guess what his master wanted. He spoke several languages fluently and was intelligent. When the position of valet at the residence of the British ambassador Sir Hugh came up, Cicero got the job. But what Sir Hugh didn't know was that his new manservant had other interests that were going to prove counterproductive.

One was photography. Another was the maid at the embassy, and the third was snooping around embassy files. Cicero learned that his new master was a man of habit. Everything in Sir Hugh's life was run like clockwork. He brushed his teeth twice a day. He always played the piano after lunch, and he had his meals at the same times of the day. When he drove his purple Rolls Royce, he knew exactly when he was leaving and when he would return. Another of Sir Hugh's habits was that he liked to read top-secret documents in his residence and kept them in the safe.

One evening while Sir Hugh was having his bath. Cicero slipped into his bedroom on the excuse of laying out his evening clothes and made a wax impression of his personal safe key. He had a friend make a replica of the key, and after that, everything Sir Hugh kept in a safe was given a thorough reading by his manservant. This was a perfect routine, and the more Cicero snooped, the more daring he became. He even started to give Sir Hugh sleeping pills, so he could read and photograph his secret papers left on a bedside table.

Fantastic secrets were inside: plans to launch air attacks from Turkey against Romania. There were details of meetings between American President Roosevelt and British Prime Minister Churchill and Soviet leader Stalin. But best of all, Cicero passed on news of the forthcoming Allied invasion of Europe. Cicero even gave us its codename—*Operation Overlord*—but the German High Command still believed this information was too good to be true.

They believed Cicero was genuine, but the information he supplied was fake. Nazi high command thought it was planted by British intelligence for him to find and pass on to the Germans. Cicero told me that he cared little for what the Germans did with his information and even less of what they thought of it as long as the money kept coming. His money piled up. He hid it under his carpet in his bedroom. He didn't save any money and spent extravagantly. He rented a country cottage and equipped it with every modern convenience. Cicero even called it *Villa Cicero* after his German codename and had a little plaque put up above his door. He and his girlfriend became regular customers at one of the most fashionable clothing shops in all of Turkey. Their clothes and jewels would have shamed even the high society socialites.

I was irritated with the way Cicero flaunted his wealth and warned him about his poor decisions, especially when I saw him wearing a gold watch. Even his girlfriend, who believed he was working for the Turks started to chide him. I once overheard her say:

"People are going to wonder about how we can afford such wonderful clothes, you're only a valet after all."

He smiled at her and said:

"Don't you worry, they're all too stupid."

But in fact, they weren't. It was the Turks who first started to take an interest in Cicero. Turkey was neutral in the war. As the conflict dragged on, they wondered which side would best suit their own interests to support.

One night after Cicero dropped off more film at the German Embassy. I drove him home and noticed a large black car following us. I sped up the car, and he sped up to keep close. I was desperate to shake them off. I hit the accelerator and sped through Ankara's fashionable Boulevard at over 100 miles an hour. Later that week, I bumped into a Turkish official, he said:

"My dear man. You really are a most reckless driver. You should take more care, especially at night."

It was a warning and the first hint that Cicero's spying days were numbered. More alarming events followed. At the British Embassy, a team of security experts arrived to install a security system for the ambassador's secret documents. Cicero heard Sir Hugh discussing the system with one of these men and was able to work out a way of bypassing it. It didn't stop the secrets that continued to flow from the British embassy to Germany.

Cicero was about to be given away by a spy of far greater daring than he was in the German Foreign Ministry. A man named Fritz was a German who hated the Nazis. Fritz had direct access to all the material that Cicero supplied the Germans in Ankara. Fritz alerted the Americans and then told the British that they had a spy loose inside their embassy. British intelligence couldn't figure out who Cicero was until he was betrayed from within the German Embassy.

I had a grumpy, unproductive secretary named Nellie. She was a 20-year-old blonde that pouted and sulked her way through the entire working day. She was lazy, and I wanted to get rid of her. The only reason I couldn't was that her father was a high-ranking German diplomat. Nellie, for all her faults, did at least show an interest in my work. This was because she was also a spy. She worked for the OSS. The American Office of Strategic Services and managed to get a key cut to fit my safe. She photocopied everything that passed through it.

Before long, she knew that Cicero was really Eleyza Bazna. It was now the end of March 1944, and Nellie decided it was time to escape. If I were to find out that she was a spy at the German Embassy, she would've been tortured and shot. But she was able to get away. She cut her hair, dyed it black, and took a plane out of Turkey.

The British Secret Service wasn't sure Cicero was their man, so they set a trap. One night, a British security officer settled down in Sir Hugh's office with a glass of whiskey and switched the lights off. The door opened, and the light came on and there stood Cicero, key in hand. The two men looked at each other, but not a word was said. Cicero turned and left—it was over for him. He couldn't be arrested because he hadn't broken any Turkish laws. He had an argument with a furious Sir Hugh. He rounded up his possessions, including all the money under his carpet. Then he left the embassy for good. He decided to lay low in one of Ankara's exclusive districts.

My secretary had vanished under suspicious circumstances, and now my first agent had been discovered. The German High Command in Berlin was extremely displeased with me and send me a stream of telegrams demanding my immediate return to Germany. I was afraid for my life. I needed to buy some time. I telegraphed back that I was ill and unable to travel. The next day I received a call at my house. A mysterious voice said:

"I'm calling on behalf of the British, if you go back to Germany, you will be shot, come over to us and save your life."

It was an awful dilemma to be in. I was reluctant to betray my country. I was a loyal national socialist and had joined the party before Hitler even came to power. Even now, I still believed in our cause. But as luck would have it, I never had to decide. Shortly after the Allies invaded France —as Cicero predicted—the world turned against Germany. The Turks took this as a cue to join the allies. All German diplomats, including myself, were arrested and detained for the rest of the war.

I heard that Cicero was extremely pleased with himself. He was still alive and fabulously wealthy. He took the £300,000 he'd saved and went off to Portugal and then South America. Here, the world turned sour for him.

Bankers turned up at a luxury villa he'd rented and told him that all the banknotes he placed within the bank were counterfeit. Cicero took the news in good spirits and laughed out loud at the deception. The Germans decided his information was useless, and they weren't going to pay any real money for it.

What followed was far from funny for Cicero. He was arrested and sent to prison for passing forged banknotes. When he was released, he headed back to Germany to ask the West German government to compensate him for his earnings.

Predictably, his request was not successful. He died poor and alone in Istanbul, 1971.

OPERATION VALKYRIE

I t was a spring morning in 1943. The roar of American fighter planes screamed low over the Tunisian coastal road. They unleashed machine-gun fire into our column of German Army vehicles.

I felt the heat from the explosion and watched the fierce flames bellow up from the blazing trucks. I stared into the smeared blue desert sky, covered in a cloud of black, oily smoke. I blinked and tried to keep my eyes open. I was badly wounded and fought for my life. I was brought to a Munich hospital and given the best possible treatment.

My left eye, right hand, and two fingers from my left hand were lost in this vicious attack. My legs were so badly damaged that the doctors told me I could never walk again. I willed myself back from the brink of death. I was determined not to be defeated by my injuries. I refused all painkilling drugs and learned to dress, bathe, and write with my three remaining fingers. My recovery was astounding, and before the summer was over. I demanded to be returned to my regiment.

The hospital staff was amazed by my stubborn persistence. They admired what they thought was my patriotic determination to return to active service. But my determination was not to fight for Nazi leader Adolf Hitler. What I wanted to do was kill him. I had supported the Nazis once, but my experience in the war turned me against them.

I watched in Poland as SS soldiers murdered innocent Jewish women and children by the roadside. When I fought in France, I watched a Nazi field commander order the execution of dozens of unarmed British prisoners. But the worst things I've ever seen were what Hitler's war had done to the Soviet Union. Our invasion was fought with such great brutality against Russian soldiers and civilians. I was also sickened by Hitler's incompetent interference in the campaign, and his stubborn refusal to allow exhausted troops in impossible situations to surrender.

After one disaster of a battle, I asked a close friend:

"Is there no officer in Hitler's headquarters capable of shooting him in the head?"

I laid in my hospital bed and realized I was the man for this job. I knew I had my flaws. I could be untidy in my personal appearance, but I was incredibly strict about punctuality and orderliness. I knew I had a ferocious temper. I could become enraged over the smallest thing—like an aide laying out my uniform—less than perfect. But I was also blessed with a magnetic personality and was told I was a brilliant commander. I had a natural sensitive nature and encouraged my fellow officers to confide in me. All these aspects of my character made me an ideal leader to oppose Hitler.

When the hospital allowed me to leave, I was appointed Chief of Staff in the Home Army. The Home Army was a unit of the German army made up of all the soldiers stationed in Germany. It was also responsible for recruitment and training. I quickly established that a deputy commander of the Home Army, General Olbricht, was not a supporter of Hitler either. He offered to help me overthrow him. Between the two of us, we began to persuade other officers to join us. My fellow conspirators and I soon devised an ingenious plan to get rid of Hitler. In the previous year, the Nazis had set up a strategy called *Operation Valkyrie*.

It was a precaution against an uprising in Germany against them. If there was a revolt that broke out the Home Army had detailed instructions on how to seize control of all areas of government—important radio and railway stations —so that the rebellion could be quickly put down. But rather than protect the Nazis, we intended to use *Operation Valkyrie* to overthrow them. We planned to kill Hitler. And in the confusion that followed his death, set *Operation Valkyrie* in motion and order all the soldiers to arrest Nazi leaders and their chief supporters, especially the Gestapo and the SS.

Our plot had two flaws. Killing Hitler was difficult; he was always surrounded by bodyguards. When we approached General Fromm, he refused to take part. He was like everyone else in the armed forces that had sworn an oath of loyalty to Hitler, and he used this as an excuse for not betraying him. He feared Hitler's revenge if the plot failed. Without General Fromm's help, using *Operation Valkyrie* to overthrow the Nazis would be difficult. But we weren't deterred. We threw ourselves into the task of recruiting allies—many officers joined us—many more wavered. Many were disgusted by the way he led the German Army, but like Fromm, they felt restrained by their oath of loyalty or feared for their lives if our plot should fail.

We were careful to avoid being discovered by the Gestapo. We typed our documents wearing gloves to avoid leaving fingerprints on typewriters that would be hidden in a clipboard or an attic. I memorized and then destroyed the written messages and left not a scrap of solid evidence against us. My judgment in recruiting conspirators was so good that not a single German officer I approached to join our conspiracy betrayed us.

In the summer of 1944, time was beginning to run out. The Gestapo began to suspect a significant revolt against Hitler was being planned. They searched hard for any conspirators and evidence to condemn them. The longer the conspirators delayed, the greater the chance of being discovered. We decided the best way to kill Hitler would be to do it with a bomb placed in a briefcase. As part of my Home Army duties, I attended conferences with the German leader. He believed I was a glamorous figure and had high regard for my abilities. Because I had such close contact with Hitler, I volunteered to plant the bomb myself. To give me time to escape the bomb, we primed for a 10-minute fuse.

To activate the bomb, a small glass tube containing acid needed to be broke with a pair of pliers. This acid would eat through a thin steel wire. When this broke, the bomb would detonate. On July 11, I went to Hitler's headquarters in East Prussia for a meeting with Hitler and two other Nazis. Herman Göring and Heinrich Himmler. I wanted to kill all three, but when Himmler and Göring canceled. I decided to wait for a better opportunity.

My next chance was on July 15th. I was again summoned to Rastenburg. I set *Operation Valkyrie* into motion before the meeting. But at the last second, Hitler decided not to attend the conference where I was going to plant my briefcase bomb. I made frantic phone calls to Berlin to call off *Operation Valkyrie,* and the conspirators covered their tracks by pretending it had been an army exercise.

Our chance came on July 20, 1944, when I was summoned to Hitler's headquarters at Rastenburg. I was joined by my personal assistant, Lieutenant Haeften. He picked up two bombs and drove to the airfield south of Berlin. From there, he took a three-hour flight to Rastenburg. We arrived in East Prussia at 10:15 a.m. and drove through the gloomy forest to Hitler's headquarters. It was surrounded by barbed wire checkpoints and minefields— the base was known as the *Wolf's Lair*. It was a collection of concrete bunkers and wooden huts cut off from the real world.

Hitler retreated here to wage his final battles of the war. Our conference with Hitler was scheduled for 12:30 p.m., and at 12:15 p.m., the conference began to assemble. I requested permission to wash and change my shirt. It was such a hot day that this seemed like a perfectly reasonable request. I was ushered into a nearby bathroom where I was joined by my aide Haeften. We began to activate the two bombs. I broke the acid tube fuse on one, but as I reached for the second bomb. I was interrupted by a Sergeant telling me to hurry and that I was late for the conference.

One bomb would have to do, and there was more bad news. I'd hoped the meeting was to be held in an underground bunker. A blast of this bomb in a windowless concrete room would mean certain death for all inside, but instead, I was led to a wooden hut with three large windows. This meant the force of an explosion in here would be much less effective.

The conference had already begun inside the hut. High ranking officers and their assistants crowded around a large oak map table, discussing the progress of the war in Russia. My hearing had been damaged when I was wounded, and I asked if I could stand next to Hitler so I could hear him properly. I placed myself next to Hitler, on his right and shoved my bulging briefcase under the table to the left of a large wooden support pillar. Less than seven minutes remained before the bomb was due to explode. I had no intention of staying inside the hut. Luckily for me, the discussion about the Russian front continued, and I made an excuse to leave the room, saying I had to make an urgent phone call to Berlin.

General Keitel was already irritated by my late arrival and became infuriated that I'd had the arrogance to leave the conference. He called after me, insisting that I stay. I ignored him and hurried away. Like all our fellow conspirators, we hated Field Marshal Keitel. We called him—*Lakeitel*—which meant lackey in German. It was now less than five minutes. I hurried over to another hut and waited with my friend. General Fellgiebel, the chief of signals at the base, one of several Rastenburg officers who'd joined our conspiracy. The seconds dragged by like hours.

Inside the conference room was an officer named Colonel Brandt, who came over the table to get a better look at the map. His foot caught on my heavy briefcase. He picked it up and moved it to the opposite side of the heavy wooden support. Seconds later the bomb went off. My aide Haeften drove up in a staff car and I leapt in. We drove fast to escape to the airfield before the *Wolf's Lair* was sealed off by Hitler's guards.

We drove past the devastated hut and felt confident that no one inside could have survived. But we were wrong. Brandt and three others had been killed moving the briefcase to the other side of the wooden support. But he'd shielded Hitler from the full force of the blast. The German leader staggered out of the hut. His clothes were in tatters and his hair was smoldering, but he was still alive.

Hitler's death was an essential part of our plot. Shortly before one o'clock. I sent a message to the War Office in Berlin, confirming that the bomb had exploded. I ordered General Olbricht to set *Operation Valkyrie* into motion. I made no mention of whether Hitler was alive or dead. But back in Berlin, General Olbricht hesitated because he wasn't sure if Hitler was killed.

He decided to wait until he knew more, and he was not prepared to act. I was still flying back to Berlin and was cut off from everything. During the two hours I was in the air, I had expected my fellow conspirators to be following through with *Operation Valkyrie* and there to be a frenzy of activity happening. Nothing happened. It was unfortunate I couldn't have been in two places at once. I was the best man to carry out the bomb attack in Rastenburg. But I was also the best man to have directed *Operation Valkyrie* in Berlin.

At Rastenburg, it didn't take long to realize who planted the bomb. Orders were immediately issued to arrest me at Berlin's Rangsdorf airfield. But the signals officer responsible for sending the message was one of our conspirators, and he never transmitted the order. It was an hour and a half later at 3:30 p.m. before the Berlin conspirators began to act.

The Home Army officers were summoned by General Olbricht. He told them Hitler was dead and that *Operation Valkyrie* was to be set in motion. General Fromm still refused to cooperate. He called Rastenburg and was told by General Keitel that Hitler was still alive. It was now 4:30 p.m., and the conspirators issued orders to the entire German Army. Hitler, they declared was dead. Nazi leaders were trying to seize power for themselves. The Army was to take control of the government immediately to stop them from doing this. I arrived back in Berlin not long afterward. I again failed to persuade General Fromm to join our conspiracy. He erupted into a foaming tirade against me. He banged his fists on the desk and demanded that we be placed under arrest. He ordered me to shoot myself. When General Fromm lunged at one of our officers with his fists flailing, we subdued him and pressed a pistol into his stomach. He meekly allowed himself to be locked in an office with other officers of the Home Army Headquarters, still loyal to the Nazis.

I began to direct the conspirators with my usual energy for the rest of the afternoon. We worked with desperate haste to carry out our plan. I spent hours on the phone trying to persuade any wavering Army commanders to support us. I was convinced Hitler was dead, but many people I spoke to wouldn't believe me. It was widely believed that the Nazi leader employed a double who looked and acted just like him. What if I killed the double rather than the real Hitler?

From Paris to Prague, the army attempted to take control and arrest all the Nazi Party command officials. Cities like Paris and Vienna were successes, but in Berlin, it was another story. Here we were foiled by our own decency. We'd revolted against the brutality of the Nazi regime. And, in retrospect, if we'd have taken a similar ruthlessness—it might have saved us. If we'd been prepared to shoot anyone who stood in our way, we might've succeeded. We also failed to capture Berlin's radio station and other army communication bases in the capital.

All through the late afternoon, our own commands were contradicted by orders from commanders loyal to the Nazis.

It was now early evening, and it became evident that our plot had failed. I refused to give up. I insisted our success was assured and continued to encourage my fellow conspirators not to give up hope.

The end was near. Hostile troops loyal to Hitler surrounded the War Office. Inside the building, a small group of Nazi officers armed themselves and set out to arrest us. Shots were fired, and I was hit in the shoulder.

General Fromm could only do one thing. He'd refused to cooperate with the conspiracy. Still, he'd known all about the plot, and no doubt the conspirators would confirm this under torture or even their own free will. He had to cover his tracks. He sentenced us to immediate execution. I still bled profusely from my wound, and I didn't care about a death sentence. I insisted the plot was entirely my doing, and my fellow officers had only carried out my orders. General Fromm was having none of this.

Just after midnight, we were hustled down the stairs to the courtyard outside. We were placed against the wall, lit by the dimming lights of a staff car. The four of us lined up in order of rank. I was second after General Olbricht. Before I was cut down—in a brave but pointless gesture—my aide Haeften threw himself in front of the bullets and died at my feet.

There would have been more executions that night, had not the Gestapo chief arrived and put a stop to them. He was far more interested in seeing what could be learned from the conspirators who were still alive. The Gestapo torturers were cheated out of their greatest prize. My fellow martyrs and I were buried in a nearby churchyard. We failed, but in our bravery and in the face of such a slim chance of success, we'd been truly heroic. If we'd succeeded, *Operation Valkyrie* and the war in Europe might have ended much earlier. It continued for another year. In those final months of the Second World War, more people were killed than in the previous five years of fighting.

Hitler described the *Operation Valkyrie* conspiracy as a crime unparalleled in German history. Although we were already dead and buried, Hitler demanded our bodies be dug up, burned, and the ashes scattered to the wind. The main surviving conspirators were hauled before the Nazi courts. They also refused to be intimidated. Knowing the regime they loved was teetering on the brink of defeat.

General Fellgiebel, who'd stood with me as the bomb exploded in Rastenburg, was told by the court president that he was to be hanged. He replied:

> *"Hurry with the hanging Mr. President, otherwise you'll hang before I do."*

Gestapo and SS officers continued to investigate the plot until the end of the war. They made over 7,000 arrests and over 2,500 people were executed. One of them was General Fromm. Although he never joined the conspirators, he was shot for cowardice and failing to prevent them from carrying out their revolt.

HERO OF BUDAPEST

I was from one of the most prominent families in Sweden. I came from a long line of bankers, diplomats, military men, and politicians. I was a curious kid, sensitive, gentle, but also fearless. I remember how much I hated fox hunting. Once, I let all the dogs on my family's estate escape a night before a hunt.

My family was determined to see me become a banker, but I was more interested in trade and architecture. I attended Michigan University in the United States, where I assisted my girlfriend and worked with physically handicapped children. In the 30s, I went to Haifa, Palestine, where I met Jewish refugees fleeing from the Nazis.

On my return to Sweden, I set up a successful import-export business called the European trading company with my Hungarian Jewish partner. After the Second World War started. Sweden was neutral. This meant that I was able to travel around Germany, her allies, and all the conquered territory cutting business deals with the Nazis and their collaborators. I often went to Budapest on these work visits.

Because of my influence and connections, I was asked to

help secure documents for Jews trapped in Nazi-occupied territory. I agreed to try and set off toward Hungary by train at once. On July 9, 1944. I had with me over $100,000 donated by the American Jewish charities. I knew what the Germans intended to do to the Jews, and I understood the bizarre mentality of high-ranking Nazi officials.

The men that ruled Germany and its conquered territories believed that destroying the Jews was more important than defeating the approaching Soviet Army. These men were corrupt, and generally open to whatever bribes I could throw their way. It was a bizarre combination, and it created a small corridor of opportunity which I could operate in. I was well known for plenty of business trips to occupied Europe and I also understood how to handle the low-ranking officials. Policemen and ordinary soldiers had a deep fear and exaggerated respect for authority. This gave me an inherent advantage.

I was tall and well-spoken. As a polyglot, I spoke four languages: Swedish, German, Russian, and English. I was known as a wealthy aristocrat from a prominent Swedish family, which gave me a natural air of authority, and I used it to my benefit. Here in Budapest was my perfect example of a man and his circumstances matching perfectly. My sensitivity, decency and keen knowledge of the human character allowed me to survive in what would soon be known as a treacherous madhouse.

I enlisted the help of other Swedish diplomats and we immediately set about creating a fictitious Swedish citizenship. It was a protective pass, known as a *Schutzpass*. The Budapest Swedes had already tried to make similar passes, but my design was an enormous improvement. I knew how much the Hungarians and Nazis admired impressive-looking documents, and I cooked up a formidable-looking pass in yellow and blue. It had a coat of arms, official signatures, stamps, as well as the three-crown symbol of Sweden. I was given permission to manufacture over 5,000 of these passes but made 20,000. We created other meaningless identification documents just so we could wave them at the guards and police.

These passes declared the holder was in the process of emigrating to Sweden as a Swedish citizen, and that the protection offered by this pass should be extended for the holders' family. Shortly after I arrived in Hungary, I came across Adolf Eichmann for the first time. We arranged to meet in a nightclub in Budapest in August. It was in this meeting that I offered to buy a substantial amount of Nazi property in the capital. He knew what I wanted these buildings for. I wanted them to provide sanctuary for the Jews, and he brushed aside my offer. He was unimpressed with me and dismissed me as a soft, diplomat.

Eichmann met resistance on his proposed deportations from several sides. The Hungarian leadership no longer had the power they wielded before German troops took over the country, but still tried to protect the Hungarian Jews. Various factions in the Nazi party squabbled about how to carry out all the deportations and what delayed their implementation. Because of this, the deportations were put on hold and Eichmann returned to Germany.

It was now early autumn and my efforts to protect the Hungarian Jews had been successful. I contemplated returning home. But events took a turn for the worse. The puppet leader of Hungary, Admiral Horthy, became convinced Hungary should withdraw from the war. On October 15[th,] there was a pre-recorded speech from him broadcast on the Hungarian national radio that announced the end of the war. The speech was greeted with delight and people danced in the streets. But Admiral Horthy underestimated the ruthless determination of the Nazis.

In only minutes after the broadcast finished, another announcement was made. This claimed that Hungary was still in the war and the airwaves were filled with the sound of patriotic Nazi songs. An instant change of heart was brought on because the SS troops had kidnapped Admiral Horthy's son. They threatened to execute him unless the Admiral changed his mind immediately. Admiral Horthy stepped down as a leader and went into exile in Bavaria. His son was sent to a concentration camp and the fascist Arrow Cross party took control of the country.

The new government immediately announced that they'd no longer recognize the Swedish *Schutzpass*. But I still had another trick up my sleeve. I was friendly with another young Austrian aristocrat, who had recently married the new Hungarian foreign minister. I told her about the Jews being deported and exterminated. I explained that if her new husband allowed this to happen, he'd be hanged after the war as part of the government that had permitted this type of atrocity to happen. She talked to her husband and persuaded him to recognize the Swedish *Schutzpass*. But now with Admiral Horthy gone, armed thugs of the Arrow Cross were unleashed to murder Jews on the streets.

Eichmann and his SS troops returned, and Jewish community leaders were summoned to a meeting with him:

> *"You see I'm back again,"* he hissed like some type of pantomime villain. *"You forget that Hungary is still in the shadow of the Reich. My arms are long, and I can reach the Jews of Budapest as well."*

The deportations began again. At this stage of the war

the massive resources that were once available to the Nazis were no longer theirs to command. The Russians were fast approaching from the East. And they destroyed rail links, trains, and freight wagons. Fuel was scarce. But Eichmann's determination was unstoppable. When the trains couldn't be found to transport Jews, they were marched out of Budapest instead. In a few autumn dark days, over 80,000 Jews were rounded up in Budapest and marched out of the capital to Austria. The Jews that departed from Budapest usually went straight to Auschwitz. But this group was earmarked to be worked to death at the armament factories.

If anyone faltered on their march, they were shot where they stood. Others froze to death during the overnight stops or died from exhaustion. But whenever the columns of Jews were marched off, I followed behind with food and medical supplies. I'd hand out protective passes and always managed to bring back at least a few hundred people from the thousands who left. I was scared, and I pushed through with inner courage. I'd rush into a crowd of frightened Jews assembled for deportation, under the bayonets and rifles, of jittery ill-tempered soldiers. I would shout:

"Who has Swedish papers?"

while handing them out to those around me.

Sometimes I'd arrive at a train packed with Jews en route to Auschwitz. I'd stand in front of the train to prevent it from leaving. I'd climb on the roof of the freight cars, handing out my Swedish *Schutzpasses* to anyone that appeared through the narrow slots at the sides. Sometimes I stuffed bundles of passes into the trains. Occasionally, I would be pushed around by the guards, and even had warning shots fired above my head. I did not have any official right to behave as

I did. Still, I always acted as if I had complete authority, like a man whose orders should not be disobeyed.

It was early November and I met Eichmann again face to face, this time at the Gestapo headquarters in Budapest. He greeted me with open hostility and threats. I presented him with my gifts of Scotch whiskey and cigarettes. Unlike many of the Nazi High Command, he wasn't someone who could easily be bribed. I'd guessed that the vanity of this man from a humble background would be tickled by a gift from a Swedish aristocrat. We shared a drink and he became friendlier. He even offered to divert a small trainload of Jews to Sweden in exchange for ransom. But I didn't trust him. And Eichmann's feelings toward me rapidly turned murderous. A few days after the meeting, a German military truck attempted to ram my car. It failed. After that, I made it a point of regularly changing the house where I slept.

I used money provided to me by the US War Refugee Board and set up an international ghetto. There were rows of houses, 72 and all, with over 15,000 Jews sheltered in them. I'd find Jewish men who looked particularly *Aryan* and dressed them in stolen SS uniforms to stand guard outside houses. Other diplomats followed my example from Portugal, Spain, and Switzerland, who also provided safe havens and rented buildings to become hiding places for the Jews. All throughout November, as the cold central European winter settled on the capital, the deportations and killings continued. The Russian troops approached fast, and an air of anarchy overtook Budapest.

Any semblance of law and order evaporated. The Arrow Cross thugs and Nazi troops knew full well that their days were numbered. In their twisted ideology, Jews were considered the source of their troubles. And in their final days of power, they worked around the clock to kill as many Jews as they could. Swedish delegation houses were broken into, and any Jews hiding inside were massacred.

Eichmann declared:

"I know the war is lost, but I'm still going to win my war."

Despite Eichmann's attempts on my life, I decided it was still worth inviting him to dinner to make one final bid at stopping him in his plan. In December, we had our last encounter. It was an arranged meeting and we had other dinner guests. We met in a hilltop mansion that overlooked Budapest. It was a strange and theatrical evening. Wine and fine food were served on elegant China dishes, and a cordial atmosphere was established. After the meal, we returned to the sitting room for brandy and cigars. The room had a fantastic view of the city. It was a well-documented scene that could have easily come from a Hollywood movie. I pulled back the curtains and revealed the horizon lit up with flashes of artillery and rockets from the encroaching Soviet army.

"Look how close the Russians are," I said to Eichmann. *"The war is finished; the Nazis are doomed. Those who cling to this hatred until the end will be hanged. It's the end of the Nazis, the end of Hitler and the end of Eichmann."*

Eichmann replied:

"I agree. I've never agreed with all of Hitler's ideology, but it has given me a good career. I understand that this comfortable life will soon end. No more planes bringing

*wine and women from France, the Russians will take my
dogs, horses, and my mansion—probably shoot me as
soon as they find me."* Eichmann continued, *"for me,
there's no escape and no freedom. There are however
some consolations. If I continue to kill my enemy...when I
finally walk to the gallows. I'll know I've completed my
duty."*

The Germans left soon after. I was thanked for an exceptionally interesting and charming evening. Eichmann
sneered and said, "don't think we're friends because we're
not. I plan to do everything I can to keep you from saving
your Jews. Your diplomatic passport will not protect you
from everything, even a neutral diplomat can meet with an
accident."

It was now Christmas Eve, and the Russian troops were
at the gates of Budapest. Eichmann fled, but his final order
was for that the remaining 80,000 Jews of Budapest to be
rounded up and executed. The German general in charge of
defending the capital mustered over 500 men and armed
them with heavy machine guns. I was alerted to this forthcoming massacre. I sent word to the general that I would
hold him personally responsible and see to it that he was
hanged when the war was over. He called off the massacre
just minutes before it was due to begin.

On January 13, the Soviet troops arrived on the outskirts
of Budapest. I was ecstatic and believed my troubles were
finally over. For months I've risked my life against
extraordinary odds and survived. But it was only now, when
with a supposedly friendly army that my luck deserted me.
It was my own negativity, which had allowed me to act with
such bravery that betrayed me.

I had grand plans for post-war Budapest, and I outlined

them to the Soviet officers. I had an idea to help the Jews after the war. They invited me to discuss matters further behind the Russian lines, and we drove away from the capital in a Red Army truck. My friends in Budapest and Sweden were never to see me again. The Russian High Command believed I was an American spy. They arrested me and held me in the infamous Lubyanka prison in Moscow, home of the feared Soviet secret police.

I had one chance to return home and that came in 1946. When the outgoing Swedish ambassador in Moscow was summoned for a final meeting with Soviet dictator Joseph Stalin. Stalin asked him if he had any special requests. The Swedish Ambassador asked if I was still in Soviet hands, and if I was, could they release me. But then the ambassador admitted to Stalin that he thought I was dead.

He might as well have signed my death sentence. Stalin was just as ruthless as Hitler, if not worse. If the Swedish government thought I was dead, it would be far simpler to kill me then to admit I had been wrongly imprisoned. I was executed in my Moscow cell on July 17, 1947. I devoted my life to stopping the work of an evil regime. But another set of circumstances conspired against me, and I became one of the first victims of the Cold War. A sullen peace between the Soviets and the Western Allies followed the destruction of Nazi Germany.

The war produced more than its fair share of senseless moments, but for a man who had saved over 100,000 lives through his own ingenuity and courage, it was an unjust fate.

IWO JIMA

When I think of the Pacific Islands, I conjure up comforting images of white sand beaches, sunshine and an endless horizon of blue seas. Not on Iwo Jima. It's a bleak volcanic slab of scrubby vegetation and black ash, shaped like an overloaded ice cream cone that's frequently lashed with driving rain.

Iwo Jima means sulfur Island. It's that evil-smelling chemical similar to rotten eggs. It emanates from the dormant volcano that makes up the glowering hillside in the southern tip. The island is only eight square miles and it takes about five minutes to drive across it. During the war, many Pacific Islands inhabited by Japanese soldiers were cut off from supplies by the allies and left to surrender or starve.

Iwo Jima was a notable exception. The island had two Japanese Air Force bases inland from the stone and ash beaches. From here, our fighter planes could pound the factories and cities of mainland Japan. When we took Iwo Jima, we'd provide these bombers with a closer base to Japan, especially for the emergency landings on the return journey.

The battle for Iwo Jima was one of the fiercest in the Pacific. The soldiers of Imperial Japan, since the 30s, had fought to build a Japanese Empire in the Pacific. They conquered territories that were once part of the fading European empire. These soldiers fought with suicidal cruelty and infamous bravery. They had only contempt for enemy soldiers who surrendered even if defeat seemed inevitable. When Japanese soldiers faced certain capture, they'd rather kill themselves than fall into enemy hands.

We fought with unquestionable bravery, but it was not our culture to sacrifice ourselves needlessly if defeat was inevitable. We'd been at war with Japan since 1941 when they bombed Pearl Harbor. Admiral Yamamoto, the architect of that attack, who was never convinced in its wisdom, stated:

> *"I fear we have only succeeded in awakening a sleeping tiger."*

He was right. We were one of the wealthiest, most powerful nations on earth. When war broke out, our country devoted our entire resources to fighting. The invasion fleet sent to attack Iwo Jima was extraordinary. It was over 70 miles long. We had over 850 warships with almost 300,000 men. A third of them were intended to fight on the island itself. The Japanese knew the strength of their enemy. Several diplomats and senior soldiers in the Japanese High Command had lived in America before the war.

The commander of Hiroshima, General Kuribayashi, was one of them. His strategy to defend the tiny island was effective but grim. He ordered his outgunned 20,000 soldiers with no hope of rescue to stand to the last man on an island that was sure to fall. He reminded them that they had a sacred duty to defend this Japanese territory to the death. Every soldier was instructed to kill at least 10 Americans before they perished.

General Kuribayashi and his masters in Japan knew that the US troops were heading toward the mainland intent on conquering Japan. They hoped that the American losses on Iwo Jima would be appalling. Causing the American public to force President Roosevelt to come up with a peace treaty to prevent an invasion and national humiliation. In the months before the invasion, Iwo Jima was turned into a fortress, concrete gun emplacements, pillboxes, and scattered machine gun nests dug into the mountain littered the island. Every cave was full of soldiers, and there was an intricate network of tunnels underneath that linked them up. There were underground hospitals large enough to treat over 500 wounded men. The Japanese soldiers weren't on Iwo Jima—they were in it. I later read that in no other area in the history of warfare was as skillfully fortified by nature and by man.

We were sent to seize this tiny island with the third, fourth, fifth, and 21st divisions of the US Marines. The Marines prided themselves on their skill of amphibious assaults, fierce fighting, and intense loyalty. But the majority of those sent to Iwo Jima had never been in combat before. Most were like me, still boys of 18 or 19. We were about to be thrown into one of the most savage battles of the history of warfare. At an age when other young men would still be grappling with their first year of college, or even in high school, with their first love, or first job. Most had still not yet left home. There were boys younger than 16. Some were 16 and 17, who'd lied about their age when they were recruited. It wasn't a surprise when these boys died at the point of a Japanese bayonet or were blown in half by a mortar shell.

The facade of manly toughness seared away and their last words were often a desperate, frantic cry to their mothers.

We began the attack on the morning of February 19th. The sunrise was pink in a pale blue sky. Before we started our invasion, we spent a sleepless night in preparation for the assault. Our day began at three in the morning. We were fed steak and eggs for breakfast. Then, after 7 a.m., we filed off to our enormous troop transport ships down metal steps to fill the holds of the smaller landing craft that would take us to the island. I heard a fellow soldier who'd never been in combat recall some sarcastic advice he received from another soldier. He said:

> *"You don't know what's going to happen. You'll learn more in the first five minutes here than in the whole year of training you've been through before coming to Iwo Jima."*

Naval shelling of the island stopped at nine o'clock in the morning. Five minutes later, clumsy amphibious tanks emerged from the landing craft onto the soft beaches, which ran for over two miles down the south side of the island. They drove underneath the hateful gaze of Mount Suribachi. The invasion was only two minutes behind the carefully planned schedule.

Fear clutched my heart. As we approached the enemy shoreline, an intense blast of adrenaline pulsed through my body. I knew when the heavy steel door at the front of my landing craft lowered onto the frothing sea at the edge of the beach. I'd be exposed to machine-gun fire and possibly ripped to shreds. That is if I hadn't been already blown up by a shell before my boat reached the shore.

When the doors of the first wave went down, we were

greeted by the smell of rotten eggs and sulfur. The shells from our ships and planes were whistling over our heads onto the island. We saw no Japanese. At first, I assumed because of the 75-day bombardment of the island by the US Navy and carrier aircraft; they might have wiped out the Japanese defenders.

I later found out General Kuribayashi had ordered his men to hold their fire while the beach filled up with American troops, tanks, and supplies. It was a full hour before the Japanese bombardment began after we started our invasion, and it was catastrophic. Through the chaos of disembarking tanks, bulldozers, and Caterpillar tractors around the beach, a lethal rain of bullets, shells, and mortar fire fell on us. I remember that Mount Suribachi lit up like a Christmas tree only instead of tinsel and lights, it was hellfire and guns. The whole mountainside turned into a fortress. Seven stories of fire platforms and gun emplacements were hollowed out of its interior. There was nowhere to hide.

We hugged the soft sand as bullets flew so low they ripped our clothes and supplies in our backpacks to shreds. The loss of life was hideous. My fellow soldiers were torn apart by shells. Their bodies spread all over the beach. Even some of the hardened NCOs vomited in horror. Others caught directly by explosive shells were vaporized, no trace left of human remains. I yelled over to my Sergeant and asked him if this was a bad battle in the heat of the fighting. He shouted back:

"It's a slaughter!"

In less than three seconds, he was blown to pieces by a mortar.

I remember thinking that Iwo Jima was like running

through rain and not getting wet. I later read that the life expectancy of a soldier in the battle was less than 20 seconds. In that first hour of shelling, the success of the invasion hung in the balance. It took a terrible toll. Several things about Iwo Jima made it especially horrifying. The intensity of the Japanese bombardment made it not matter if a soldier hid in a fox hole or charged up open land, he'd be killed. We only saw our Japanese adversaries after we killed them. Most of the time, we were fired on by an unseen foe who could see us, but we couldn't see them.

Once we were off the beach, we headed into thin scrub and grasses. It was terrain peppered with pillboxes, caves, rocks, and blockhouses, all of which sheltered the Japanese soldiers. We attacked the Japanese with machine-gun fire, flame throwers, and grenades. The tunnel system they'd built underneath the mountain linked their strong points. That meant when we neutralized a blockhouse, it would become quickly lethal again with other Japanese soldiers crawling through the tunnels shooting at our backs.

Even through the slaughter, we were winning. The horrific opening bombardment had not driven us off the beach. And by now 10,000 more Marines had come ashore. By mid-morning, one company from the 20th Marine Regiment had managed to cross the 700 yards that separated the furthest Southern landing from the islands Western shore. Their casualties were immense. Of the 250 men in the company, only 37 still stood. That night the fighting faded, and over 30,000 men had managed to come ashore.

By now, we were exhausted and laid huddled in shallow holes and trenches Japanese soldiers snuck through the darkness to try and murder us. The next morning brought fierce winds and high seas, making any further landings impossible. Other Marine forces began to cautiously to infiltrate the Northern interior of the island, and the grand plan for the day was to attack Mount Suribachi itself.

I was one of the 3,000 Marines of the 28th regiment. On that day, we edged up to the base of the mountain. The weather on the third morning of the island brought no relief. It was going to be a grim day to die. As we prepared for our assault, an artillery barrage from behind our lines opened up for an hour. Navy carrier planes went into plaster the mountain with rockets. The designated hour of the attack came, but no order to advance was given. We've were promised tanks to protect us as we ran over the open ground toward the tangle of vegetation that covered the base of Mount Suribachi.

There were no tanks available for us. Without tanks, our losses would be far worse than we were already expecting. They were short of shells and fuel. So, Marine High Command decided the attack would go on anyway. The order was passed, and the regiment was ordered to charge forward without tanks. A feeling of dread swept through me. A fellow soldier reminded me that this would be like his father's slaughterhouse when cattle realize they were about to be killed.

I summoned all my inner courage. The fear was like a physical weight bearing down on me. I broke cover and ran toward the mountain slope. I expected to be cut down in seconds. As I ran, I saw hundreds of other Marines behind me and to the side of me. Mount Suribachi erupted into a dazzling flash of fire, bullets, and shells raining down on the charging Marines. We had been trained to advance at all costs.

We gradually reached the base of the mountain. The man to my right fell, his legs were peppered with shrapnel. I took cover behind a rock and tried to treat his wounds until a medic arrived and gave him pain-killing morphine. I continued forward, trying to destroy the blockhouses and machine guns that lay at the foot of Mount Suribachi.

When the men with flame throwers were able to get close enough to do their hideous work, tanks eventually appeared to help our assault. The Japanese defenders on the mountain began to crumble. Throughout the day of fighting, the companies and platoons of the regiment inched further and further up the mountain. By nightfall, we had even penetrated behind Japanese lines. We laid low amid the parachute flares and searchlights from offshore ships that came out in penetrating brilliance.

Every moving shadow was potentially an approaching Japanese soldier. On the fourth day, we continued to creep forward, sometimes hearing the enemy in tunnels and the command post beneath us. More often than not, only locating a Japanese strong point, when a hill of fire was unleashed on them. Now, we had strong artillery and tank support. The Japanese defenders inside the mountain were burned and blown into oblivion.

In the fading light, the Japanese soldiers became aware that they were cut off from retreat and tried to stage a breakout. Over 200 Japanese soldiers broke cover and desperately dashed down the mountain, only to be slaughtered. We got our first sight of the soldiers who had rained such hell on us. We counted less than 25 that made it back to the Japanese lines. On the fifth day, our morale boosted immensely. The fighting strength of the Japanese soldiers inside Mount Suribachi was gone. It was now possible to capture the mountain outright. If the Marine command was wrong, it could prove to be a very costly gamble.

Our days fighting began with another air attack. US Navy planes smothered the top of the mountain with napalm. After that, the mountain seemed quiet. I wondered if all the remaining Japanese had fled. There was only one way to find out. I was part of a four-man patrol sent to summit the mountain's 550-foot peak. Every footstep could bring death, but the enemy never fired on us.

The Marine High Command decided to risk a 40-man platoon. As our platoon snaked higher up the mountain, we caught the eye of every man on the beach. We expected the remaining Japanese on the mountain to open up and cut us to ribbons. Our platoon advanced with great caution. Every cave we passed, someone tossed in a grenade in case it contained enemy troops. And after a tense half-hour, we stood breathless at the top, not quite believing that we were still alive.

At 10:20 a.m., we raised the stars and stripes and used a piece of drainage pipe as a flagpole. When the flag went up, a huge cheer rose from the throats of thousands of Marines watching below. The warships offshore sounded their horns, and the men onboard hollered in triumph. Even though the fighting was far from over, seeing the American flag flying over Iwo Jima was the highest point of the battle. It convinced every Marine that we were there to stay. We stood around the flag and posed for the Army photographer. The flag fluttered in a stiff breeze as we stood out on top of the mountain. I'll never forget that day. I also remember thinking that we were now a target for every enemy sniper and artilleryman within range. It was like standing in the middle of a bullseye.

The noise from raising the flag alerted the Japanese. The ragged Japanese soldiers emerged from their hiding places. They fired rounds at us and tossed grenades. We dove for cover and shot back. Amazingly, no one was hurt, and the mountains settled down again in silence. Several hundred troops remained on Mount Suribachi, but they had all lost the will to carry on. Most of the Japanese soldiers chose to kill themselves rather than fight to the death or surrender.

Mount Suribachi may have been the most strategically useful spot on the island, but its conquest was symbolic. Another month of slow, agonizing fighting dragged on before the 20,000 men under General Kuribayashi's command were finally wiped out. Less than 200 taken prisoner. The last of these surrendered in 1949 when he found a scrap of newspaper reporting on the American occupation of Japan. The remaining Japanese soldiers hid in the maze of defensive tunnels inside the mountain. For nearly four years, they ate food from US Army supplies to keep from starving.

Our casualties were horrific. For the Marines that landed on the first day, nearly 6,000 were killed, and over 17,000 were wounded. General Kuribayashi's Japanese soldiers sold their lives for at least one or two American deaths. Survival seemed a matter of luck. I fought for 36 days and was injured several times. I survived a nighttime sword attack. I woke up to hear a Japanese soldier attacking the soldier next to me. On another occasion, as I talked to a soldier, he was shot in the face in mid-conversation.

After the battle on a troopship home, I was haunted by nightmares of combat. Once, I woke to find myself strangling the man in the next bunk. The Battle of Iwo Jima served its purpose. Japanese fighter planes no longer harassed American bombers that passed over the island.

In the final months of the war, over 2,000 damaged *B-29s*, which would otherwise have crashed into the sea, were able to land. This saved over 27,000 US Airmen onboard these huge bombers from certain death.

TICKLING THE DRAGON

I led a team of scientists who'd constructed and detonated the first atomic bomb. It was the *Manhattan Project*, and it was a costly and complex undertaking. My team had three huge problems. We had to create material to make a bomb, ensure that it worked, and then perfect a method of delivering this weapon to its target.

We started with an initial budget of $6,000 in February 1940. We'd escalated our budget to over $1.5 billion by the summer of 1945. Getting our project started had been difficult. Most people were baffled by the process of atomic physics. The subject was alien. Scientists bidding for government funds would explain, for example, that each atom of uranium contained 200 million volts of electricity.

Officials greeted this information with open mouth disbelief and scorn. It was only because of a letter from Albert Einstein that eventually persuaded the US government to begin funding research into the atomic bomb. By 1945, those on my team working on the project included some of the most distinguished scientists from America, Britain and Canada. My team also contains several refugees from Fascist Italy and Nazi Germany and other occupied countries in Europe.

Since the beginning of the century, it was known that powerful forces lurked within atoms. During the 1930s, scientists in Germany and America discovered the process of nuclear fission, where atoms are split apart to release energy. It soon became clear that the process could be used to create an immensely powerful bomb. But only a few materials are suitable for fission. One is uranium 235 obtainable from uranium ore. Another is plutonium, an entirely man-made material produced inside a nuclear reactor.

Acquiring even small amounts of these substances is a costly, difficult, and time-consuming process. It involved massive amounts of electrical power. Both plutonium and uranium 235 are such powerful explosives that a sphere of either material the size of an orange would produce a detonation equivalent to over 20,000 tons of TNT. The most used explosive in artillery shells and bombs.

The process of developing this dangerous weapon was complicated. Some of my team referred to their experiments as *tickling the dragon*. But due to the skill and caution used by our world-class scientists, there were no fatal disasters during development. It was now the summer of 1945, and the Manhattan Project had developed two kinds of bombs. One was known as the gun type. This would produce a nuclear explosion by firing a small piece of uranium into a larger piece. The other kind was known as the implosion-type. This fired several high explosive charges into a plutonium core.

In terms of factories, development labs, research, natural resources, and manpower, my operation almost matched the scale of the United States car industry. Even though we employed over 600,000 people, it was still top secret. Vice President Harry Truman only found out about the Manhattan Project after he became president in 1945.

It was fear that drove the American government to fund such a vast enterprise. Fear that the Japanese and Germans would produce a similar weapon before we did. Once the fission process had been discovered, it was only a matter of time before someone would produce an atomic bomb. Fortunately for the world, Japan and Germany never even got close to developing a workable bomb. We didn't realize this until the war was over. Hitler's rabid anti-Semitism excluded many gifted German Jewish scientists from German universities. He was indifferent to the consequences. Hitler said:

> *"If the dismissal of Jewish scientists meant the annihilation of contemporary German science, we shall do so without science for a few years."*

Even though German nuclear physicists had made essential discoveries during the 30s and 40s, they were hampered by a lack of funding. In 1943, just to make sure, British commandos destroyed a German laboratory in Norway, where atomic research was being carried out. The Japanese lacked both the funding and resources to ever stand a serious chance of developing their own weapon.

I was not entirely likable. I was skinny, tall, and told I had a mischievous pixie-like face. I was known to have an unpleasant humor and at times, I could be sarcastic. Before the war began, I established a reputation as one of the greatest scientists of my age, despite flaws in my character. I managed to build a brilliant team of scientists at the California Institute of Technology. I did much the same with the Manhattan Project. I was an American Jew and especially driven to produce such a weapon before the Germans did.

My scientific studies encompassed both the tiny atomic particles and the vast black holes. I didn't stop there. Along with neutron stars and positrons. I also had space left in my brain for French literature, music, art, and politics. My politics often brought me trouble. Most of my family and close friends, including my girlfriend, were active left-wing radicals and even communists. This was unusual in America in the 30s, especially among the more liberal-minded academics and students. I was never a communist. But my career was stalled several times by government officials who said I'd betray our atomic weapons to Soviet Russia.

* * *

I was on the crew of the *B-29 Superfortress, Enola Gay,* and we were stationed at Tinian airbase in the Mariana Islands in the Pacific. By the time the atomic bomb was ready to be used. Germany had already been defeated. Japan still held on fighting fiercely, even though she had zero chance of winning the war. It was April 1945, and our troops had landed on the Japanese island of Okinawa and fought for 82 days against a fanatical resistance.

Our leaders feared an invasion of the Japanese mainland would cost more than half a million American lives. Our new atomic bomb was ready, and it was decided that it was to be used. We gave the Japanese government an ultimatum, warning them of the prompt and utter destruction of their country if they didn't surrender. We debated on whether we should provide a demonstration to the Japanese or just let them know what the bomb could do.

This demonstration idea was rejected. We targeted the

industrial city of Hiroshima in the south of Japan as our first target. The reason for its selection was that it had been barely touched by previous bombing raids. It'd be easy to determine how much damage had been caused directly by the atomic bomb.

We were chosen to deliver the most destructive device ever produced. We were told that the bomb about to be dropped was something new in the history of warfare. A man came directly from the *Manhattan Project* to oversee our mission. He persuaded the commanding officer to let him finish assembling the bomb once we were in the air. The previous day we'd watched half a dozen *B-29s* crash taking off from Tinian. Such a crash with a fully activated bomb would have wiped out the entire island in one blinding flash. We were dangerously overloaded with our menacing cargo as we struggled off the runway, barely avoiding crashing into the sea. Flying alongside us were two other *B-29s* packed with scientific instruments and cameras. It was 2:45 a.m. on August 6th.

Barely 15 minutes into the 1,500-mile flight, the observer from the Manhattan Project climbed down the steel ladder into *Enola Gay's* bomb bay. He inserted the explosive charges into the bomb, which had been given the codename *Little Boy*. It was fully assembled a few hours later, just as the sun was coming up over the North Pacific. He replaced the three green plugs in the bomb with three red ones. *Little boy* was now armed and ready, and our pilot chose this moment to inform the rest of the crew that we were carrying the world's first atomic bomb.

It was now 8:12 a.m., and we began our bombing run. The sight of three tiny silver *B-29s*, high above Hiroshima could hardly cause any distress. The city went about its early morning business as usual. In the glass nose of the aircraft, the bombardier peered through his bomb site and called out small directional commands. The plane was heading directly for the Aioi bridge in the middle of the city. The bridge formed a distinctive T shape that linked an island in the Ohta river with the city on either side of its banks.

At 8:15 a.m., we saw the bridge appear directly in the lines of the gunner's site. The bomb was released from the plane. We were immediately much lighter, and our plane lurched up into the air. *Little Boy* carried a message from the ship that delivered it.

Greetings to the Emperor from the men of the Indianapolis.

The bomb plummeted to Hiroshima. It had a three-stage detonation sequence to guard against any premature explosions. The first switch was triggered when it left the plane. The second was activated by the air pressure when it reached 5,000 feet. The third, which would set it off, was operated by an onboard radar set to register at 1,890 ft above ground. This was considered the height at which it would do the greatest damage.

Little Boy was a uranium gun-type bomb different in design from the one that exploded in the original desert test. Such a bomb had never been tested. It was possible that it wouldn't work. But it did work, at 8:16 a.m. 43 seconds after it had fallen from the *B-29*, *Little Boy*. It exploded over a hospital 820 feet off target instantaneously. At 5,400 degrees Fahrenheit, half the temperature of the surface of the sun. Buildings and people vanished. In some places, shadows were all that remained of some Hiroshima residents. Their outlines caught on a wall or pavement for a fraction of a second before their bodies were vaporized. Birds fell from the sky in flames. Buildings were flattened and people caught in the open turned into charcoal statues, their fingertips glowing with an eerie blue flame.

A mile from the explosion, a train of commuters was flung from the track like a discarded toy. In the first seconds after the bomb exploded, over 80,000 people were killed. The air rushed back to replace the blown away air from the initial blast. This created a hurricane-force tornado that sucked people into the rubble of its swirling dark heart. Once we'd recovered from the shockwave that tossed our plane like a cork on a wave, we gazed down in wonder. The city looked like it was a pot of boiling black oil. It was a bubbling mass with a red core. Two-thirds of the city had been destroyed.

When the fires died down, a black ash rain and radioactive dust fell in the weeks and years to come. Over another 90,000 Hiroshima residents died of radiation poisoning. The same day we called on Japan to surrender. The President warned:

"A reign of ruin from the air, the like of which has never been seen on Earth."

But the Japanese were too stunned to react. Hiroshima had been isolated, and accurate reports of its fate could not be sent to Tokyo. When the news did reach Japan's leaders, it was considered a wild exaggeration. On August 9th, another bomb was dropped. This time on the city of Nagasaki. It was a plutonium implosion-type device. It had much the same effect as the Hiroshima bomb, both in the damage that it caused, and the number of people killed.

Japanese leaders, especially the war minister, argued that the war should continue. Emperor Hirohito intervened to stop the fighting. He said:

"The time has come when we must bear the unbearable."

Army officers tried to stage a coup to continue the war. It failed. Most of the Japanese High Command committed ritual suicide, together with scores of other high-ranking soldiers who could not bear the shame of defeat. The fighting stopped on August 15th. On September 2nd, the Japanese government ministers went aboard the USS Missouri anchored in Tokyo Bay and signed the surrender documents.

It was six years and a day after the Second World War had begun. The dropping of atomic bombs on Nagasaki and Hiroshima were two of the most significant events of the war. At the time, the decision provoked a heated debate among our military and political leaders. But for the ordinary American soldier, the bombs were a fantastic release.

When the bomb dropped, news began to circulate that the invasion of Japan wouldn't take place after all. We cried with relief and joy. We were going to live. We were going to grow to adulthood after all.

AUTHOR'S NOTE

Without a doubt, these were the most horrific conflicts ever fought. Despite the scale of the wars, their hardships and astronomical casualties, many people who lived through it, look back on it as the most significant days of their lives. It was the battlefront campaigns, the front line or home front camaraderie, wartime romance and eventual victory.

This excitement and camaraderie was often bought at a terrible price. Many soldiers who fought in these wars never spoke about their experiences to their friends and family. For years after, many took to drink to dull the grief they felt for their fallen brothers, or to blot out the memories of the terrible things they'd done to other men. Survivors of the war sometimes felt a heavy grief and guilt for having come home alive when so many other men had perished.

Those who fought, and those who lost family and friends like to think that they were fighting for a better tomorrow. The Cold War that followed WWII and the nuclear standoff between the Soviet Union and the United States was a bleak end to the conflict. But the idea of a world controlled by Imperial Japan and the inhuman regime of Nazi Germany is truly a haunting one.

My goal in writing this book is twofold. First, it's meant to entertain and teach about a time in history that we should never forget. We should always keep the memories of these deeds fresh in our minds, so we can never allow them to be repeated.

Second, I believe we can teach history from a story-teller's perspective. Instead of rote memorization of endless facts, figures, names and places, why not show what happened from those in the trenches, skies and on the seas? This is the type of history and story that I plan to tell. If you enjoyed reading this book, I encourage you to write a review. Also, visit WarHistoryJournals.com to view our other extraordinary stories from 20th century conflicts and battles.

ALSO BY WAR HISTORY JOURNALS

Mongoose Bravo: Vietnam: A Time of Reflection Over Event so Long Ago

"A frank, real, memoir" – Reviewer

Uncover the gritty, real-life story of a Vietnam combat veteran.

With an engaging and authentic retelling of his experiences as an infantry soldier of the B Co., $1/5^{th}$ 1st Cavalry Division in the Vietnam War, this gripping account details the life and struggles of war in a strange and foreign country.

Broken Wings: WWI Fighter Ace's Story of Escape and Survival

"A masterfully told story of triumph and redemption in a powerfully drawn survival epic." – Reviewer

Hero WWI Fighter Pilot Shot Down and Captured.

With an engaging and authentic retelling of his experiences as an escaped prisoner of war, this gripping account details the life and struggles of a captured pilot in 1917 war-torn Europe.

Lieutenant John Ryan couldn't wait to see action in WWI. He joined up with the British colors out of Canada. As one of several American pilots in the Royal Flying Corps before the US joined the war, he earned his wings and became an Ace through fierce air battles over the skies of Germany.

War on Influenza 1918: History, Causes and Treatment of the World's Most Lethal Pandemic

"A remarkable yet frightening history that serves as a stark warning of the threat of pandemic flu." – Reviewer

Influenza should scare you.

Read Into this detailed and chilling account of the Influenza outbreak of 1918. A terrifying virus that stretched across the globe. Even now, a century after the great flu of 1918, which left an estimated 50 to 100 million people dead worldwide, there's still no cure.

This book examines influenza from all sorts of angles—history, diagnosis and treatment, economics and epidemiology, health-care policy, and prevention, and it gives insights on pandemics.